Praise for *Activate Your Brain*

"If you want one book about how to put your best brain forward, read *Activate Your Brain*. Scott Halford has written a fascinating neuro spin on success that teaches you how to consciously create your most productive brain and to optimize your interactions with others. He expertly ties together behavioral psychology and his own practical training method with a characteristic sharp, funny style. *Activate Your Brain* is altogether perfect!"

—Mary Case, MD, neuropathologist

"Most of my days are spent trying to figure out what's going on in other people's brains. Now I have a better understanding of my own. This is a groundbreaking book for the layperson who wants to unleash the power within!"

—Mark Madgett, Senior Vice President of Agency Distribution, New York Life Insurance Company

"Scott Halford is one of the world's only thought leaders who truly understands both business success principles and the neuroscience of the brain. In this book, he combines them to bring you a powerful guide for how to take your life and business to the next level!"

—Rory Vaden, cofounder of Southwestern Consulting and *New York Times* best-selling author of *Take the Stairs* and *Procrastinate on Purpose*

"Scott understands how the human brain functions and turns that into forceful action. His ability to speak to the real potential of the brain and unleash the secrets of using it to its fullest is unmatched. He makes business people revolutionize their thinking, which quickly changes how they behave."

—Patti Dennis, Vice President of Talent Development and Recruiting, Gannett Company

"A compelling look into how to harness the power of your brain to do, have, and become more."

—Randy Gage, author of the *New York Times* best seller *Risky Is the New Safe*

"I encourage you to read *Activate Your Brain*, love it, and buy a copy for anyone with whom you want to work more effectively or whom you love and want to see enjoy life more. If everyone understood the contents of this book, the world would be a better place. This is the science of being successfully you."

—Amy Brann, author of *Make Your Brain Work* and
Neuroscience for Coaches, Director of Synaptic Potential

"Scott Halford serves as your executive coach and guides you on a journey through the lens of how your brain influences professional and lifestyle choices. *Activate Your Brain* is written in Scott's naturally warm and funny voice and is a must-read if you are looking to develop your core performance skills and emotional intelligence."

—Geil Browning, PhD, founder of Emergenetics International

"This fast-moving, enjoyable book is loaded with great ideas that you can use immediately to think with greater clarity, make better decisions, and unlock more of your inborn potential."

—Brian Tracy, success expert and international best-selling author
of *Now, Build a Great Business* and *No Excuses!*

"*Activate Your Brain* translates much of the knowledge scientists have discovered about the brain in the last 20 years into practical actions that we can take to *be* more and to *accomplish* more—with less stress. Written with the busy business person in mind, this is not only a truly fascinating read but also a hands-on guide to living a more complete life."

—Bill Cates, President, Referral Coach International

"I love this book! *Activate Your Brain* is easily accessible, true to brain science, and incorporates important psychological and neuroscience research. It will improve your life. Start small, start now, and buy this book."

—John B. Molidor, PhD, Professor of Psychiatry, Michigan State University
College of Human Medicine; author of *Crazy Good Interviewing*

"Scott Halford knows that becoming a great leader requires you to be emotionally aware and fully intellectually engaged. Read *Activate Your Brain* and learn how."

—Colleen Abdoulah, Chair, WOW!, Internet, cable, and phone provider

Activate
Your Brain

How Understanding Your Brain
Can Improve Your Work—
and Your Life

Scott G. Halford

GREENLEAF
BOOK GROUP PRESS

Published by Greenleaf Book Group Press
Austin, Texas
www.gbgpress.com

Distributed by Greenleaf Book Group

For ordering information or special discounts for bulk purchases, please contact Greenleaf Book Group at PO Box 91869, Austin, TX 78709, 512.891.6100.

Design and composition by Greenleaf Book Group and Debbie Berne
Cover design by Greenleaf Book Group and Debbie Berne
Cover image: iStockphoto/VLADGRIN

Publisher's Cataloging Publication Data is available.

ISBN: 978-1-62634-197-5

Part of the Tree Neutral® program, which offsets the number of trees consumed in the production and printing of this book by taking proactive steps, such as planting trees in direct proportion to the number of trees used: www.treeneutral.com

Printed in the United States of America on acid-free paper

15 16 17 18 19 20   10 9 8 7 6 5 4 3 2 1

First Edition

Other Edition(s):
eBook ISBN: 978-1-62634-198-2

CONTENTS

Activating Your Brain

WARNING: The following paragraph may make you feel uncomfortable.

You have a work deadline staring at you. It's a day before you need to deliver. You're tired and crabby with your friends and family, but you believe they understand, because you're under pressure and once it's over you'll be back to your charming self. You work furiously into the wee hours of the night, until you become so weary that you drop into a fitful sleep with your laptop next to you in bed. You awaken with a start a couple of hours later because you inconveniently remember something you forgot. Your groggy brain is convinced that it's the biggest deal in the whole wide world. You look at your alarm clock and feel a sense of dread because it's three in the morning and you only have three more hours, at the most, to sleep. The anxiety keeps you awake, but you're too tired to get out of bed and make progress on your project. You eventually fall back to sleep, sort of. When your alarm goes off, you can't believe how tired, how *off*, you feel. You get up and go about your morning activities before work, hoping that your partner or kids or dog doesn't require any of your cognitive power, because you really don't have any left. You get to work, open your scads of emails, and begin your day of distractions and worry.

It's just another day in the life of a stress junkie. The scenario is always different—a volunteer commitment you really don't have the time for, the addition of a new leadership initiative to your already full plate, a request (read: demand) from an out-of-touch boss—but it plays out again and again in many people's lives. If that is you—occasionally, sometimes, or often—I bet you feel overwhelmed, exhausted, and out of control. I can risk that bet because I've experienced this scenario myself and hear about it from the majority of the professionals I talk with in my work. What's disturbing to me is when they follow their laments with statements like "Oh well, there's nothing I can do about it" or "I don't really have a choice."

Many of us feel victim to our circumstances. We *have to* work sixty or seventy hours a week or we might not get noticed and win the next promotion. We *have to* commit to every school activity or our kids will grow up to be criminals. We *have to* tackle another house renovation or our neighbors will think we're derelicts. We have to, we have to, we have to.

Yet, I would bet (another safe risk) that what your company really wants is for you to be in control. Your family and friends do too. They may not have said those words to you, but they want you to be healthy, happy, productive, and engaged in your life. Sounds wonderful, right? Achieving those glorious goals requires taking control, because control is a main driver in activating the full potential of your brain and changing your behavior. Amazingly, small changes—slight alterations in the choices we make—can have a dramatic effect on our sense of control. Over time, those small choices build into more dramatic shifts, and then suddenly, you can't believe how different your life is. We've all heard not to sweat the small stuff, but I respectfully disagree. It's the small stuff that actually leads to the energy, inspiration, and motivation it takes to accomplish great things.

Throughout this book, I'm going to help you discover the small, easy choices you can start making today that will help you activate your full brain and achieve the productive, effective, fulfilling life we all want. I won't "should" you, and I won't criticize. What I hope to do is share knowledge and some realities that will empower you to "start small, start now"—the mantra of this book.

THE BRAIN, YOUR CAPTAIN

Stradivarius violins, especially those made by Antonio Stradivari in the seventeenth and eighteenth centuries, are considered unrivaled in their quality and sound. In 2011, a Stradivarius in pristine condition sold for around fifteen million dollars. Imagine if a violinist took one of these instruments onstage, acknowledged the audience, and then smashed the Strad to pieces before she sat down and tried to play. That's utterly absurd, of course. And yet we all own something far more valuable than a Stradivarius—a brain—and many of us, over time, abuse it and then expect it to perform at stunning velocity. Our instrument deserves more tenderness and compassion than we would give a beautiful violin. This book will get us on that track.

Your brain is the captain of who you are. It dictates every action and behavior. In this book, we'll paint a picture of the productive, effective life we all want, and we'll see that the key to achieving it is the fully activated brain, and all the choices we make about its inputs—everything we put into the holes in our head (what we look at, what we eat, who and what we listen to, and so on). Those choices say much about how we go about our everyday work and life. With the inputs you choose, you're affecting your life—whether you're making it better or worse, more harried or calmer. When you understand the nature of your brain better, you can take charge of life, and live by design and not by default. You'll know which choices to make to help you feel better about who you are, to increase your energy levels, to improve your creativity, to heighten your intelligence, and to enrich the impact you have on others. That is an invigorating notion.

The small steps you'll learn to take in this book—the ones that can reduce your stress level, increase your energy, and lead to greater happiness and contentment—all rely on your awareness of how our brain operates on a moment-to-moment basis. It all starts with awareness; when you have that, you can take small steps now to create the results you want.

I would be extremely wealthy if I had a hundred dollars for every leadership and success process I've studied and tried. Most promise success, productivity, well-being, and so on. But most also ignore one essential fact: that the human brain already knows how to help us succeed. We just have to get out of the way, or at least proactively involve our brain in our success. Your brain knows the business of our species, and all of the courses on the latest strategic workflow process won't teach us what our brain is aching to do for us if we'll simply pay attention to it.

My goal with this book is to give you an awareness of the powerful little device harbored in your skull, so you can feel more in control and less negatively stressed on a minute-by-minute and even second-by-second basis. All of us get the same 86,400 seconds each day, and the tiny abuses and compassions we give our brains in those seconds affect everything we do—at work, at home, at church, while we're volunteering, while we're watching our kids' soccer games. The quality of those seconds determines the quality of our minutes, hours, weeks, months, and years. This is a book about shaking hands with your brain and getting to know how it works; when you do that, you can make the most of all of your seconds.

All of us have a brain, but this book is most focused on the brains of businesspeople: those who conduct the commerce of the world, the ones toiling every day to make some kind of difference, whether they're making data understandable to shareholders and investors, inventing technology that will save lives, or leading and inspiring others. I focus on businesspeople because they face a daily bombardment of distractions that can lead to brain-performance crises, which lead to overall well-being crises. It's a terrible pattern, but even the busiest and highest-level professionals can benefit from taking small steps—and starting now—to repair and grow their brains.

There's already plenty of "neuroliterature" out there, but the bits of it that apply to businesspeople are strewn about in many incredible books and academic articles (see the back of this book for examples). I am not a neuroscientist, but I have formally and informally studied the brain for years—and I felt it was time to collect all that information in one place. This book isn't exhaustive or deeply technical, of course, but it draws a bead on the neural concepts I have found to be useful to all of us businesspeople on our voyage to making each one of our seconds count.

Here's what the book is hopefully *not* going to do. It's not going to shame you. The last thing you need is another book on what you're not doing right or how to be more of something you're not even sure you want to be. If you're like me, you probably get tired of feeling like you're not keeping up with all of the "requirements" of a successful person. Equally tiresome is that ever-growing yardstick of being more productive, getting more out of life, having more—blah, blah, blah. The people I talk to—around the world—look at me with recognition when I bring this up, as if I've discovered some deep, dark secret we all share. It can sometimes feel lonely trying to keep up with the frantic pace of business life, but you'll discover that we are all in this together. Many of us are saddled with "impostor syndrome"—we have that voice that says, "Oh my gosh, what if they find out that I don't know what they think I know?" Well, consider this to be a respite from all that, a sort of spa for your brain and your mind. By letting go of all that pressure and worry, and instead making deliberate, brain-friendly choices, you're much more likely to do more and have more. By the time you finish this book, I believe you'll take away a new appreciation—and maybe even adoration—of your brain. You'll see it as the priceless instrument that it is.

I would like this book to become a reference for you that you dog-ear (or highlight on your e-reader) and in which you skip around if you like. In the first parts of the book, you'll develop an understanding of basic neurochemistry, how we keep our memory center healthy, and how we stay interested in life. We'll explore how it is that we end up feeling out of control, regularly spending more time in our reactive and messy mammal brain than our inventive, focused human brain.

Early on we'll also learn about *activation*, a theme you'll find throughout the book. It's a neuro-spin on motivation, and one that could turn your world right side up when you use it. Activation is the "do it again" circuitry in our brain—and understanding it will lead to a more rewarding day. It will help us to sort through the many decisions we make. It helps with the marvelous feelings of completion as we execute more on the things we say we will do. Activation is an exciting and relatively simple concept that can be used every single day.

As you maneuver through the ideas in this book, you'll find many suggestions to activate the lessons in the pages in order to make them real in your life if you choose. They are small ideas to get you started, and that's mostly what it takes: getting started. Come up with your own ideas to get started, too. Do what works for you. But get started. Activity begets momentum that builds on itself and can help us feel like we're accomplishing something. (Many of the activation ideas in this book will suggest you write something down by hand; that's because it's been shown that we create better memory trails in our brain when we handwrite.[1] Handwriting is like strength training for the brain.)

After activation, we'll see how the threatened brain operates differently from the brain that feels safe—an understanding that's a game-changer for many. Next, we'll turn our attention to stamina and energy. You'll learn what's necessary to keep your brain operating when you want it to do excellent work, and that we're a step closer to having both stamina and energy when we finally harness the feeling of control. The stamina discussion includes stress, sleep, resting (including those glorious naps we all wish we had every day), food, drink, and play. We'll examine our best self and worst self, how to manage them, and how to make more and better choices about those so that we understand and take charge of our charisma and impact on others. Along the way, you'll find the brain participates in areas that could make the difference between an average and an excellent worker: things like goal setting, clear parameters, willpower, and managing distractions. It all culminates in the noblest place of all: achieving and creating significance. But even this loftiest of goals relies on our understanding of the brain and our ability to start small, and start now.

It's unlikely that all the practices in this book will work for you, but if you find even one that changes your life for the better, then the job of the book is done. Since this is a book about taking charge of your choices, you get to choose which practices you try and which you don't—think of it like a buffet. There's something here for most people.

This book is intended to excite your brain and spark a new curiosity about yourself. No book can give you complete understanding of inner workings—you have to come to that on your own—but I hope this book is the inspiration for you to do so. And I hope that while you're reading, you stop and think about how you feel about the topic we're discussing. The magic lies in what you say to yourself as you read; the experience becomes a dance between the words on the page and a new, budding awareness in your brain. It becomes a book about you because you place yourself into the conversation.

The Choice to Start:
Activation for Motivation

ACTIVATING YOUR BRAIN begins with realizing that you *do* have a say in how your life progresses. Think about the choices you have compared to the rest of the animal kingdom. If you're a deer or a dolphin, a dormouse or a dodo bird, you drink water. You eat what you can get. Your habitat is dictated by where you need to go for food. Your activities are dictated by whether you are a hunter or a forager. You may be one of those people who wishes you could come back as your dog (I do this often), but think about what you would be giving up in terms of the level of choice you have in your life!

But the choices we have as humans are amazing in their breadth and sometimes staggering in their complexity, so much so that research is dedicated to what happens when we have either too much or too little choice.[1] With choices, we feel more in control. Without them, we can feel threatened. The anticipation of making a choice is actually experienced as a reward in the brain via a powerful neurotransmitter that makes us want more.[2, 3]

The need to choose must be fed, or all manner of acting out ensues. As Martin E. P. Seligman so eloquently described decades ago, we learn helplessness when we believe that we have no options.[4] We give up and nearly shut down.

We become victims. On the flipside, those who believe they have options—who are optimistic—fare better in the world in everything from relationships and careers to health and longevity. Seeing and making choices—even if the choice is not to choose—is one of the elixirs of life.[5]

Making a choice is the signal to our brain that we are ready to begin a journey, which means choice is the first step in all change. The brain, being the completion machine it is, will help us through that journey toward change if we let it. First, we must understand how we react to the myriad choices we face daily. Then we must recognize how the smallest choices have the power to activate a new behavior, and how that activation can help us develop the inspiration we need to keep going on our journey.

Throughout this book, you will be prodded to make choices—even if your choice is not to do anything in a given situation. Even at work, where many feel like their choices are limited or made by others, we *do* have choices. If you are waiting for others to make choices for you, and if you expect them to be made with your best interests in mind, you will likely be disappointed. Don't be surprised when others don't step up and make healthy choices for you. If you're holding your breath for your boss to tell you that you need to take a few days off because you're burnt out, that probably won't happen until the situation gets far worse than it needs to.

The choices we make affect all of who we are, not just our work. You'll learn in the following chapters that who you are in your career is not separate from who you are in the rest of your life; work is just another facet of the same diamond. The choices we make at work will affect the choices we make at home, and vice versa. The things that happen to us will have an impact on how we go about business, no matter how hard we try to say, "That's just my personal life." Our brain is bathing in the events of our lives while we're trying to focus on getting our job done. Managing our choices about events that take place—even the small ones that put us in a slightly crankier or giddier mood—is critical to our impact, our significance in the world.

In this book, we're exploring brain-conscious choices: to think better, to take care of our brain, to bring order to our day, to take control and sometimes let go of that control, and—most important—to relieve the brain numbness we encounter as opposed to adding to it. If we can reframe our thinking when we're feeling overwhelmed by choices from *have to* to *get to*, the choices might not seem so frightfully difficult. And if we can focus on the simple choices right in front of us, we can begin a cascade through activation.

ACTIVATION TAKES US ONE SMALL STEP FORWARD

Imagine trading a paper clip for a house. Seems impossible, yet it happened. One day, Kyle MacDonald, a man from Vancouver, Canada, decided to see if he could, through a series of swaps, trade a red paper clip for a house. It's an amazing yearlong tale that began with a Craigslist ad. For one red paper clip, Kyle got a fish pen. Over time and a series of trades, the fish pen led to a Ski-doo snowmobile. The Ski-doo eventually led to a recording contract, which led to an afternoon with Alice Cooper, which led to a movie role courtesy of Corbin Bernsen, which led to one house in Kipling, Saskatchewan. Kyle tells the tale of the trades, of the travels, and of the people he met and the movements he started along the way in his book *One Red Paperclip*.

The small steps taken during the tale of the red paper clip are an excellent metaphor for how just about every big thing in our life begins: with a very, very small step. While choice is something our brain wants, so is completion. If we want to feel the bliss of completion, we have to take action once we have made our choice. We just have to decide to start, to activate ourselves. In this book, we've tweaked Nike's advice—"Just do it"—into our activation mantra: "Start small, start now." You just have to begin—even if you really, really, really, really don't want to.

The simplest and most crucial step we can all take in living the life we want is to start doing it now. If we wait to have all of our ducks in order, the first ducks we collected will have flown the coop by the time we get to the last ducks and it becomes a never-ending amassing of ducks. The prize goes to those who can get over being completely prepared before they begin.

If we don't start, we will have nothing to show for all of our choices or our preparedness. Start small, start now.

ACTIVATION SPARKS MOTIVATION

A sense of accomplishment often ignites the confidence we need to say, "I can achieve more if I want." Psychologist Frederick Herzberg found that among a list of motivational drivers at work—accomplishment/achievement, the work itself, earned recognition, responsibility, advancement opportunities, and personal growth—accomplishment tops the list.[6] This desire for accomplishment stems from the brain's desire for completion. Accomplishment sets up a chain of pleasure chemistry, while the lack of it does quite the opposite. To leverage the power of our pleasure chemistry, we need to activate.

Half of my garage at home serves as the dumping ground for summer items that need to be stored over the winter. They never really get completely sorted, and year after year the items are multiplying, crammed into unseen places. It's a mess, and each time I walk into the garage I have a viscerally bad reaction to it. It actually switches on a bit of anxiety because I know I need to get it organized, but I'm not. I want it done, but I do not want to be the one to do it. Alas, no one else is stepping up and there are only so many things in life you can hire others to do for you. Guilt. A voice telling me to get it done or be a loser-procrastinator. Most of us have this general low-level anxiety driven by all of those things left undone. But once we activate and start going, we're better able to keep on going. A body in motion stays in motion. And it works because our brain rewards us for completing tasks, even just the first step.

There is a place in the brain, just above your left eyebrow, that could be one of the big activators we need to get going.[7] Put your finger under your left eyebrow, close to your nose, and find the subtle notch in the bone. Just above and behind that is roughly where a big part of our motivation is activated—the medial orbitofrontal cortex, or the mOFC. Along with a complex highway of other neural architecture, it's one of the areas that activates and is involved in rewarding behavior. It sends signals to the reward centers of our brain and activates desire impulses to do the behavior again. On the opposite side of the brain around the right temple is an area called the right ventral lateral prefrontal cortex (RVLPFC). It's like a braking system; it says "Stop" when we need to stop.[8, 9]

These two areas modulate our behavior in a variety of different ways, and for our purposes, we want to positively activate the mOFC.

Armed with this information, I know that if I just put one thing in its rightful place, the neurochemistry to do more of it—the "Attaboy," "Keep going!" chemistry—will likely activate, and before you know it, I'm putting more and more in its place, and the task is completed.

Now you can see why this concept of activation could very well change your life. Envision activating at work and at home for all of the things that need to be accomplished. Activation seems to be easier when we are clear about the steps to take. There is a lesson for leaders in this. Employees will be more easily activated to achieve the enormous revenue goal the company has when they're clear on what, specifically, they can do to help achieve it. Again, do not confuse motivation with inspiration here. Once employees activate around the steps laid out for them, they may or may not become inspired, but they will likely keep going as a duty of their job when they have a clear roadmap.

Many leaders get frustrated when they feel like they have to spoon-feed the steps to employees; that it's a part of the employee's job and they should just know what to do and do it. Of course, it would be bliss if everyone was a self-starter. However, many of us are kick-starters and need a little kick in the pants to get going—and sometimes a kick to keep going. It may not be necessary to lay out every step, but clarity on the first few will certainly get the momentum rolling. Be clear and precise, and with a little direction and help, activation has a chance to take hold. If I had had someone to hold my hand and offer to get me started with the garage, I would have gotten it cleaned out a lot earlier.

Here's your first activation.

ACTIVATION

- Choose something small to experiment with on this first activation: Clean your desk off, clear out old files, clear out your email, file bills, balance your checkbook, clean a part of the garage, organize the pantry or fridge—you get the idea.

If you're already good at doing any of those, choose something that's more of a challenge for you to get done.

- Notice how you feel when you check that task off your to-do list. Do you feel energized? Remember that energy so that you can use it for fuel to achieve even bigger goals and get more control in your day-to-day life.

1

The Science of Being Successfully You

CHAPTER 1

Our Three Brains

BUSINESS STRATEGIST WILL McFARLAND once said something that resonated deeply with me: "Our success at work used to demand that we understand business acumen. That's not enough anymore. Going forward, the leaders and successful businesspeople of the world will also have an understanding of how to manage their biology. That will make the difference." All of us innately understand that our success ultimately relies on the three-pound gelatinous grayish-white blob in our head, but too often we fail to see just how much biology matters in the output of our lives. But the more we know about our biology, the more in control we can be—which is why we're starting with this chapter, a brief primer on the master of human biology: the brain.

Ninety percent of what we know about the brain we've learned in the past twenty years, and we still have only nicked the surface. The human brain is such a complex and wonderful thing that it's unlikely we'll fully understand it in our lifetime. Indeed, the science is currently being amended, altered, and in some cases out-and-out changed. Some neuroscientists devote their entire careers to researching a square-millimeter slice of the brain, research that will keep them busy into their old age.

Our overall success in the world is reliant upon our ability to manage the constant dance between two of the three "brains" we possess—the *human brain* and the *mammalian brain*. The third and oldest brain—the *reptilian brain*—operates without our assistance. Those who effectively manage those first two brains, the human and the mammalian, are more likely to achieve what they want. This is the foundation for making the types of choices that can change your life for the better. In this chapter, we'll take a look at the architecture and operations of these three basic brains. In the next chapter, we'll explore the chemical messaging and what we can do to influence it. In the final chapter of this section, we'll work to understand how our environments affect those messages and what that means for the choices we make.

And now, your brains await your acquaintance.

REPTILE, MAMMAL, HUMAN

Interpersonal neurobiologist Dr. Daniel Siegel uses an easy hand model to teach the basic anatomy of the brain. I'll walk you through it below, because it's great for understanding the relationship between the three brains, but you can go to YouTube and watch Dr. Siegel demonstrate it yourself.

Start by holding your hand in front of you with your palm facing you. Your arm represents the spinal cord that comes up into the brain. The base of your hand is the base of the brain, and includes the brain stem and other physiology that comprises our most ancient brain—the aforementioned reptilian brain. It operates the functions we don't think about, like respiration, perspiration, saliva-tion—any of the "-tions" that are automatic and autonomic. The reptilian brain automates every moment of our life, and really doesn't care how we feel about it.

Now fold your thumb to the middle of your palm, creating the number four. In our model, the thumb represents a big group of structures known as the limbic system. This is the heart of the mammalian brain. Among the many things the limbic system does is detect what is most important in our environ-ment. If something is dangerous, it puts that on top for us to deal with right away. It also notices danger's opposite—reward—and can help us connect to the highly positive elements of the environment. Like the reptilian brain, it is on 24/7, scanning the environment constantly to make sure we sense a threat and notice when something feels good too. The mammalian brain's architecture also facilitates memories and alerts us to pay attention and focus. The amygdalae in each hemisphere of the brain are part of the limbic system too; they serve as our chief relevance-detecting devices. These little almond-shaped structures detect things that are novel, surprising, rewarding, and threatening, to name a few. Snakes and spiders and dangerous things are always going to be relevant, but so are food and mates and smiling faces, given the right context. What do untrustworthy and trustworthy faces have in common? They both represent people we need to be looking out for, people that might be motivationally relevant at some point—whether it's to run away from them or to affiliate with them.[1] In essence, our amygdalae are facilitating a shift in our attention to things that are important to both our well-being and our survival.[2]

The mammalian brain has been described as the emotional center of the brain: It is not logical and, left to its own devices, it would cause us to act like an undisciplined three-year-old. Fortunately, if conditions are right, the mammalian brain has an overseer—the third brain.

The third brain, the human brain, is the captain of the ship. To complete our hand model, curl your four fingers over your thumb. Looks like a human brain, huh? That's the neocortex engulfing the mammalian brain. It's what separates us from our animal cousins in extraordinary ways. What's the difference between humans and our closest animal relative, the chimpanzee? Although there is only a tiny genetic difference—we share 98.8 percent of our DNA—our prefrontal cortices, the parts of the neocortex right behind our forehead, are very different. The prefrontal cortex (PFC) is the executive center of the brain, and it's the essence of the third brain. It thinks, reasons, analyzes, innovates, and manages the emotions that rise from the mammal part of the brain; in other words, it makes us distinctively human. This is the part of our brain that enables us to create everything in the world that is not natural—the book you're reading, your clothes, your bed. Everything we invent is conceived of in the human PFC. Our cousins closest in prefrontal cortex volume—chimpanzees— have smaller overall volume in their PFC than humans, but not by much.[3, 4] Still, they can't come close to what humans have concocted. In fact, there is no other beast on the planet that can do what we can do. The reasons for this boil down to many things, but the size and operations of the prefrontal cortex are among the biggest. That's why we must give it the respect and care it is due.

The human and mammalian brains—the neocortex and limbic system— interact with each other during every moment of our life. The PFC allows us to take time to think about things; the slowing down allows us to have a more reasonable relationship with our emotions. The interplay between these two brains is where we see the difference between businesspeople who succeed and those who fail miserably. Many people make it into great schools and get excellent jobs because they're technically smart and have high IQs, but they often derail because they never learn to help their human brain manage the mammalian brain. Eventually, the mammalian brain can destroy careers and relationships if we do not recognize how to bring the human brain online when we're feeling strongly about something, especially in times of crisis.

HOW OUR MAMMALIAN AND HUMAN BRAINS WORK TOGETHER

The emotions generated by our mammalian brain are messy, and they aren't governed by logic. They bring on automatic social responses, generated by what neuroscientist Matthew Lieberman calls the *reflexive system* or *X system* (because of the X in the word *reflexive*).[5] The brain structures involved in the X system include elements of the limbic system as well as a component of the prefrontal cortex. As its name implies, this system reacts by reflex: if you hit it, it hits you back without thinking. The X system is also what makes us react emotionally to stimuli throughout the day—like those pesky emails or texts that cause us a pang of anxiety when they pop up. (We will address this issue of emotional impulse control in chapter 6, about managing willpower and focus.)

In Lieberman's model, the X system is contrasted with the *reflective system*, or *C system*. While the X system draws mainly on the limbic system, the prefrontal cortex is the primary structure involved in the C system. The C system manages the X system into civility and appropriate choices. Left to its own devices, the X system would cause us to be aggressive and rude and messy.

When met with a total jerk, the X system in us says, "Strangle the twit!" The C system says, "Career-limiting move! Maybe we should talk it out."

Emotional intelligence (EI) is the dance between the more rational C system and the emotional X system. EI is a set of noncognitive (i.e., non-IQ) attributes, and if we have high EI, our C system is effectively cooperating with and regulating the X system. EI allows individuals to navigate the day-to-day difficulties and obstacles of life, manage their own emotions, and bring about appropriate emotions in others, all in an effort to be successful. In fact, it's a better predictor of individual workplace success and well-being in life than IQ and expertise.[6, 7]

ACTIVATION

- Think about a recent circumstance when your response to a situation was not exactly what you intended. You might have been tired, under pressure, or overwhelmed by your workload.

- Reimagine the situation with your human brain—the PFC, the C system—running the interaction. What if you had taken just a few moments before responding to allow the human brain to take control? What would your response sound like this time?

- Activate your PFC by literally waiting for about ten seconds before you respond. Take a few deep breaths and slow down. When you respond immediately, you are likely operating out of your emotional brain first, and that can be fraught with overintensity and inappropriate words. Your response regulated by your PFC will almost always be more successful.

- Avoid making big decisions when you are overly stressed or tired. That's when the emotional brain comes out to play, and you don't want that brain making important calls in your life.

Some scientists[8, 9] estimate that we spend only about 2 to 10 percent of our waking hours in the C system and the rest in the X system—which means that most of our time is spent on the animal side of nature, reacting, responding out of impulse, defaulting to the negative, and missing the positive. That's somewhat understandable: the C system is much more energy intensive to operate, while instantaneous X system reactions are less expensive to operate. In short, most of us have to work to improve our emotional intelligence. We have to decide to spend the energy. Here's where we have an opportunity. Imagine if, through awareness and new choices, we could increase the time spent in the human brain by just 1 or 2 percent. Look at what has been created in the world when the human part of the brain has been engaged, even for just short spurts. We have some incredible goals to shoot for as humans, and the activities in this book are aimed at getting us in that C system more of the time.

CHAPTER 2

Maximize Your Moments Through Your Neurochemistry

VISUALIZE THE DIFFERENCE BETWEEN a day when you're at the top of your game and a day when even the slightest nuisance sends you into a tizzy. On some days, everything falls into place no matter what the world throws our way. There are scads of emails to answer, a looming deadline, phone calls from home, curveballs from the boss, but we perform well—maybe even exceptionally well. It's like we're in a kickboxing match with the demands of everyday life, and we're fit and winning. It's exhausting, but it's a good kind of exhausting. We may even feel energized at the same time. Then tomorrow comes, and it is completely different. Even the simplest task is a struggle. Why do we have these down days, even when we're facing the same circumstances that we excelled in yesterday?

The neurochemistry of the brain has the power to alter our behavior, mood, and perspective on the same set of circumstances from day to day. In a nutshell, neurochemistry is the complicated balance of chemicals in our brain that affects how each brain structure functions, how the parts of the brain interact, and how the brain as a whole guides our behavior and responses. Neurochemistry is determined, in part, by our perception of a situation—whether we see it as a threat or something that will help us thrive. On one of those bad days, mundane challenges like deadlines, emails, and interruptions can build up and be perceived as a big threat by the brain. We then act accordingly, to protect ourselves from this threat. We can move from a positive outlook to this negative, reflexive, protective one very quickly. One moment you're humming along, but then the boss calls and puts your entire alarm system into overload. Without some intervention on your part, the mammalian brain takes over and you begin to tumble downhill.

Currently, we don't entirely understand the neurochemical changes we experience from day to day. The potential outward causes are many. You may have received bad news, slept badly, had an argument, eaten something disagreeable. (Or you might be biologically prone to mood swings. If you and your physician have determined that there is a biological cause, obviously pay attention to that.) But, we do understand the basics of neurochemistry, and developing that awareness for yourself is a good place to start retaking control of your life. With some insight, it's possible to do something about those neurochemical shifts, to lift yourself into a better state of mind and perhaps be compassionate with yourself when you need a little self-coddling.

When a good friend of mine went through the death of his fifteen-year-old dog, he admitted feeling ridiculous for feeling so intensely sad about it. He wanted to brush it off and get right back to work because it was "just a dog." There is so much wrong with that statement (dog lovers know this), but even more off-kilter is the notion that we can't give ourselves a break when something important in our life happens, regardless of what the outside world might think of how we feel about it. If you're sad, you're sad. We have a better chance of rebalancing our neurochemistry quickly if we take time to be nicer to ourselves when we're going through tough things. Even positive stress requires some self-care. My family helped me coddle myself when I was about to receive a big award. It was an immensely positive thing, but I was becoming overwhelmed by the magnitude of receiving it in front of 1,500 people. They helped me to slow down, take in the moment, and cherish the wonderful time in my life.

What follows in this chapter is a basic discussion of the physiology of emotion and behavior. Once you possess this information, you'll have more of a say in the neurochemical changes that take place in your brain and the feelings that result. You'll be able to better influence whether you will experience the good day or the bad one, and you'll make life a little sweeter in the process.

NEUROCHEMICALS AND OUR MOODS AND BEHAVIOR

The first thing to know about neurochemistry of the brain is that it's not an all-or-nothing proposition. For normal functioning, we need appropriate levels of all of our various neurochemicals. It's the Goldilocks effect applied to the brain—we need not too much of any one neurochemical, not too little of any other, but just the right amount of all of them. Any one chemical in amounts too small or great can lead to disease and even death. Many extreme neurochemical dysfunctions are out of our control, but we *can* influence many of the slight neurochemical fluctuations that happen from situation to situation by what we think, eat, drink, and do. It is important to note that every one of the neurochemicals is implicated in both positive and negative stress. We will focus on them in the manifestation of their most well-known behavioral effects.

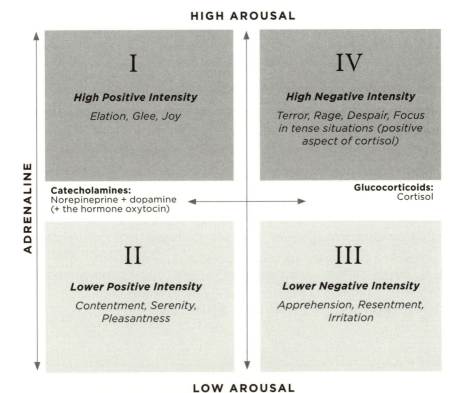

Figure 1

The graph (Figure 1) maps the primary neurochemicals and hormones involved in positive and negative feelings, thoughts, and behaviors. On the *y*-axis is adrenaline, which puts us in a state of high or low arousal or alert. In the right quadrants, we have cortisol, which is associated with stress, and in the left quadrants, we have the chemicals associated with more positive feelings: the catecholamines and oxytocin. As you can see, combinations of higher or lower amounts of certain neurochemicals create different states of mind.

We can be in so many states of mind in one day that it's, well, mind-boggling. While it's a helpful starting point to see these emotions and states of mind in neat quadrants, we're much more complex than that. For instance, you've surely experienced something bittersweet in your life. A corporate client of mine was telling me about a time when she was elevated to a position that she had long wanted, but as a result, one of her favorite colleagues had to leave the company—there was not room for them both. This woman experienced something quintessentially human: feeling elated and deflated in nearly the same breath. Sometimes those intense emotions come barreling down on us and we don't feel like we can do anything about them. (As I mentioned before, sometimes the best thing to do before responding is to wallow a little in whatever you're feeling.)

Regardless of what we experience, we do have a choice as to which of the four quadrants we spend most of our time in. The more we can understand whether we're energized or not, feeling bad or good, the more we can take steps to be in our quadrant of choice. The vast majority of the strategies and lessons of the rest of the book will hinge on your understanding of which quadrant you're in, whether you choose to be there, whether it is serving your purpose, and what to do about it if you want or need to change quadrants.

First, let's take a brief look at how neurochemicals do their job.

THE CHEMISTRY OF THREAT AND FOCUS

The brain's chief organizing principle, according to integrative neuroscientist Evian Gordon, is to maximize reward and minimize danger.[1] Fortunately and unfortunately, much more architecture in our brain is devoted to danger and threat detection than to reward detection. We need these danger-detecting brain parts; how else would our ancestors have survived all of the poisonous snakes, lethal plants, and other threats on the planet? The brain manages threat by releasing two main chemicals: adrenaline and cortisol.

Adrenaline is our "fight, flight, or freeze" hormone. High levels of it put us in a high arousal state; low levels or a lack of it put us in a low arousal state. When we perceive a threat, our adrenaline shoots up to put us into high alert, and glucose spills into our bloodstream to give us energy. Being in high arousal can lead to intense feelings, both positive and negative. High arousal is good for things like giving presentations, staying awake in a meeting, competing in sports, and so on. Low arousal is good for meditation, thinking through a spreadsheet, analyzing a business plan, or explaining algebra to a frustrated child.

The hormones cortisol and adrenaline come into play when our brain detects that we need to be highly focused and alert—perhaps to avoid an imminent threat. Cortisol is commonly thought of as the stress hormone. As with most aspects of the brain, there is an upside and a downside to cortisol. We'll get to the downside shortly, but let's look at the upside first: cortisol keeps us in the game. It keeps us awake and helps with alertness and focus. Cortisol gets us off the couch. It gives us a little bit of the edginess that researchers have discovered is "just right" for performance. Some stress hormone is essential for performing well in high-pressure situations that require quick responses to changes in the environment. Practicing the responses you want to use in high-stress situations is key because cortisol "goes looking" for the thickest pathways to fulfill what is needed to survive the moment. Think about an athlete on the field during competition. Cortisol focuses the athlete and allows access to the behaviors practiced over and over again so that in the game he will be able to display the practiced skills with greater ease. This is why professionals practice the same basic skills repeatedly.

A colleague of mine (let's call her Melissa) once consulted with a client because things had gotten really rotten in the company. Melissa sat in an executive-level meeting with the CEO and his direct reports and found herself stunned: the energy in the room could not have been less urgent or any more lackadaisical. There was a distinct lack of focus and arousal that should have been present in the room given the situation, even though these high-level employees' alarm systems should have been going off and focusing them on generating solutions. Melissa knows that when a business is being threatened by extinction, its employees had better be generating some energy and direction to get it on track again. Unfortunately, Melissa couldn't get this team to see that—their perspective on losing major clients failed to get their brains to react to the very real threat of losing important business. As of this writing, the three other clients have jumped ship.

So, the fact that cortisol helps us focus and perform when we're facing a challenge is the good part. But we can't allow too much of the stress hormone to keep us from enjoying the pleasant stuff of life. We have to get just right the right balance of cortisol in our systems for our best effectiveness. Too little and we might not have the kick in the pants we need to be competitive or to narrow our focus. But, too much and our performance can suffer, crippling us with a disorganized mind, anxiety, panic, and even paralysis.[2]

Our modern brain isn't all that different today from what it was thousands of years ago, but what we perceive as danger is very different—and that often leads to many of us living in a pool of too much cortisol. Today, most of us are able to protect ourselves from nasty beasts and poisonous snakes. The dangers are now of a different type: unmet expectations, missed deadlines, fear of looking stupid, a lack of confidence, airline upgrades given to someone else, and the list goes on for thousands and thousands of entries. Left unchecked, this daily abundance of stressors is bad for our brains and our bodies; decay and disease can be the result. Here are many of the ailments in which chronic levels of cortisol are implicated:

- the onset and progression of cancer
- the progression of autoimmune diseases such as arthritis, AIDS, lupus, Graves' disease
- immune system deficiencies
- the progression of multiple sclerosis and other neurodegenerative diseases
- high cholesterol levels
- hypertension (those shots of adrenaline, norepinephrine, and cortisol together can cause high blood pressure)

- premature aging, including wrinkling skin, graying hair, and brain shrinkage
- memory loss
- onset of diabetes

Negative Emotions: When Adrenaline and Cortisol Combine

As you see in the graph, the two quadrants on the right—III and IV—are the ones that contain negative emotions.

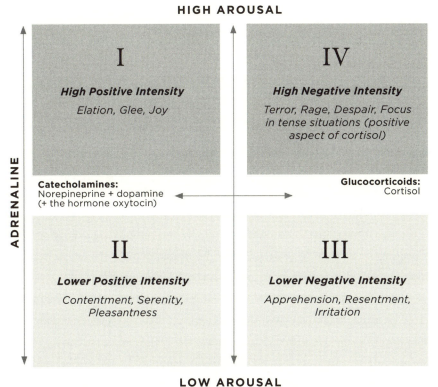

HIGH AROUSAL

I

High Positive Intensity

Elation, Glee, Joy

IV

High Negative Intensity

Terror, Rage, Despair, Focus in tense situations (positive aspect of cortisol)

Catecholamines:
Norepineprine + dopamine
(+ the hormone oxytocin)

Glucocorticoids:
Cortisol

II

Lower Positive Intensity

Contentment, Serenity, Pleasantness

III

Lower Negative Intensity

Apprehension, Resentment, Irritation

ADRENALINE

LOW AROUSAL

Figure 1

There are three basic negative emotions—anger, fear, and sadness—and all the other negative emotions found on the right side of the graph are varying intensity levels of those three. We see the intense forms—rage, terror, and despair— in quadrant IV, where the combustible combination of high arousal and high cortisol is present. The less intense forms of the three negative emotions—including resentment, frustration, vigilance, apprehension, and boredom—are found in quadrant III.

We slide into quadrant III when our thoughts become negative. Think of things that generally irritate you: unproductive meetings, emails admonishing you to do something with twenty-five people copied, someone popping in to chat while you're right in the middle of a complex spreadsheet, or the person at the checkout lane who *still* writes checks. This is the place many of us find ourselves as the day wears on and we become more tired. We get crankier, more emotional in our behaviors, and often de-energized. Unfortunately, after a very long, tiring day filled with many irritants, when we get home we may find ourselves in this quadrant.

The intense negative emotions of quadrant IV are usually big bursts of feeling and don't usually last very long. Think about a moment in your life when you got big, bad news or you were in a very bad circumstance. This could be the moment you found out you were overlooked for the job you wanted, finding out that a prospective client went with a competitor when you absolutely *knew* you had it in the bag; it could be hearing bad news about your health; it could be the moment before you plunge into a bungee jump or when someone nearly sideswipes you by cutting you off in traffic. Fortunately, we usually don't spend long in quadrant IV; by waiting and breathing before responding, we can manage the neurochemical levers downward to at least get to its less intense brother, quadrant III.

Cortisol and adrenaline interact in numerous ways to put us in quadrant III or IV. They make perceived dangers appear closer than they actually are, including looming deadlines. Our brain literally magnifies the negative, and so we get crankier and more intense. When it is stimulated, cortisol also narrows our attention so that we pay heed to what is most relevant in the environment.[3] But the focus may be so narrow that we miss other pieces of the environment when the intensity is high. In other words, the combination of cortisol and adrenaline can cloud our thinking when we need it most. Ever had a brain freeze during a presentation? It's likely because your threat levels were so high. That is an unfortunate consequence of chronic stressors. Our brain gets hijacked—blocked from doing its work, especially when it requires reason and logic—by the intense neurochemical river of negative emotions. It even happens during positive events. I received an award in front of 1,500 people in 2014. Although it was an amazing and exciting moment in my life, I literally can't remember what the audience sounded like when my name was announced. I don't remember the faces of my family and friends who were on their feet with the other 1,500 in thunderous applause (so I am told). I don't remember much of anything except trying to stay focused enough to remember a six-minute acceptance speech I needed to give.

Still, our emotions are not as out of our control as it may seem. One person can experience a major setback and crumble or become enraged, while another goes through the same event, bounces back quickly from their negative state, moves forward, and sometimes even flourishes. Think about the influences on our emotions and behavior like the primary colors at a paint store. The clerk pulls the paint levers to add a little white, a little black, a little this and that to come up with any of sixteen million different colors. The environment is one of those levers, and we usually can't control how much good or bad it gives us at any given moment. The lever we do have control over is our appraisal or perception of the event and the internal conversation we have about it.[4] If you give heavy sighs and feel frustrated when things go badly at work, if your appraisal of the situation is that there's absolutely nothing you can do about it, you'll likely have quadrant III or IV emotional responses. However, if you use your internal conversation to explore how you're feeling and what you can do to improve the situation or lessen its negative impact, you're more likely to find yourself moving toward the positive emotions of quadrants I and II.

When we live most of our lives in quadrants III and IV, we start getting used to our current state—a process known as habituation. We get used to banging our head against the wall and we no longer feel the pain, much less the concussion that will happen very soon. However, the brain likes nothing more than to get back to homeostasis—the stable, normal, unpressured state it wants to be in. All day long, it's sending us signals to help us get back to normal. If we can pause and assess, we can move toward the positive, and our brain will help us once we start.

Let's try an activation to begin the trip over to the more positive emotions.

ACTIVATION

- Next time you feel an intense negative emotion, wait ten seconds before responding (Mom was right about this one).

- Think about a situation that set you off, at work or at home. Is the situation worth the negative emotion it makes you feel? Ask yourself, "Is this really worth getting worked up over?"

- Think about how your emotions would have you respond to that situation. Would you write a rude email? Would you say something hurtful? What would have been the other person's response to your behavior? Would they have fired off another rude email back at you, or said something hurtful to you in response?

- Go ahead and write your nasty email (leave the recipient field empty!) or write out what you might have said on a piece of paper. Walk away from it for a bit. Reread it and imagine how it would have been received. Would you have come out as the winner? Now take some time to reword it less negatively. Wait another few minutes, then reread and reword if necessary. *Then* send your email or talk to the other person. Use this process for all emotionally laden communications—it will save you in so many ways.

- If you feel an amygdala hijack beginning, take a walk, even if you only have a few seconds. If you're in a meeting, excuse yourself to go to the bathroom or make up some other excuse.

It will be worth the minor embarrassment to save yourself from
responding in a way that could hurt a business relationship.

We can't and don't want to be devoid of negative emotions; they alert us
when something is wrong in the environment and help us survive. Our goal
isn't to never be in quadrants III and IV—it's to be more aware when we're there
and work to get out rather than wallowing in their neurochemical toxicity.

THE CHEMISTRY OF THRIVING

We want to perform better and feel nicer, and to have a more hopeful and pleasant outlook. When we are in these states, we can thank the neurochemistry on
the positive side of the chart—primarily the catecholamines dopamine and norepinephrine and the hormone oxytocin. Although these neurochemicals put us
in positive states, remember that because a neurochemical is good doesn't mean
that a lot of it must be great. As I described before, what we really want is the
Goldilocks effect, a "just right" combination of neurochemical levels. Too much
of even a positive neurochemical can cause damage and disease. Fortunately, we
can induce these positive neurochemicals to some degree, though not in a way
that would push us into permanent euphoria or topple us into disease (other
biological factors are often at work in disease states). Let's look at what these
positive neurochemicals—dopamine, norepinephrine, and oxytocin—do and
what we can do to experience their beneficial effects.

Catecholamines[5] are hormones that include dopamine and norepinephrine.
Dopamine is our reward transmitter;[6] it causes pleasant feelings and a sense that
we want to do something again. It's required for learning and for building neural
pathways, the building blocks of behaviors. When we refer to a dopamine bump,
we're talking about the feeling we get from a rewarding behavior. Dopamine is
essential in motor regulation, too. When the brain malfunctions and doesn't produce dopamine, that leads to Parkinson's disease and other motor disorders. Drug
abuse—primarily of drugs like heroin, cocaine, and ecstasy—can inflict permanent damage on your dopamine receptors by overstimulating them, eventually
reducing the positive effect dopamine has on your body.

Norepinephrine (also known as noradrenaline) is slightly different from its cousin adrenaline (also known as epinephrine). Norepinephrine can lead to feelings of alertness, engagement, and reward. It increases during exercise and laughter. It gets your heart pounding to increase blood flow to survive a threat, and it sparks interest and intensity.

Oxytocin is a brain-based hormone that is implicated in trust, bonding, and collaborative feelings.[7] Oxytocin is getting a lot of press these days. Neuroeconomist Paul Zak, of the University of Pennsylvania, researches and writes a good deal about it. Zak revealed that spraying oxytocin in the nose (it is not commercially available) tamped down the threat response in the amygdalae, helping individuals create a safer bonding experience and build trust with each other—critical to any good relationship. Though oxytocin is a feel-good hormone, it can also make males more aggressive when they're protecting the people (or sports teams) they love.[8]

Our Positive Chemistry in Action

The positive side of the chart is, in part, positive because of dopamine, norepinephrine, and oxytocin working within the high and low arousal states caused by adrenaline.[9]

Quadrant I is filled with intensely positive feelings like elation, bliss, ecstasy, and thrill. Think about a time in your life when you had a big burst of good feelings. Maybe you got that big promotion you were competing for. It could be getting married, the moment you saw your child born, or winning a few hundred dollars in the lottery. All of these events probably caused good feelings that were intense and relatively short-lived. The high arousal from adrenaline in these scenarios can cause us to become speechless with joy; it might also cause us to jump up and down in a show of pure ecstasy. If you've ever found yourself doing a happy dance that you might otherwise consider foolish, your catecholamines, fueled by adrenaline, were probably at work. Of course, the afterglow starts to dwindle as the event passes. If we reminisce on those intense moments, we don't often get the same pop, but we may move into another positive area—quadrant II.

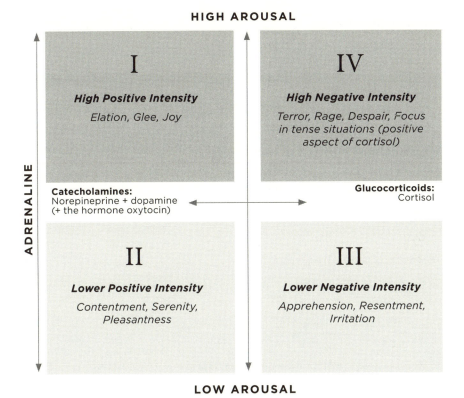

HIGH AROUSAL

I

High Positive Intensity

Elation, Glee, Joy

IV

High Negative Intensity

Terror, Rage, Despair, Focus
in tense situations (positive
aspect of cortisol)

Catecholamines:
Norepineprine + dopamine
(+ the hormone oxytocin)

Glucocorticoids:
Cortisol

II

Lower Positive Intensity

Contentment, Serenity,
Pleasantness

III

Lower Negative Intensity

Apprehension, Resentment,
Irritation

ADRENALINE

LOW AROUSAL

Figure 1

Quadrant II is the most sustainable of the quadrants, and it's the source of happiness for most of us in our lives. The feelings in this quadrant include amazement, contentment, serenity, admiration, and trust. While we may like the quadrant I intensity of skydiving or that "I just got a big raise" feeling, these boosts often rely on outside circumstances and are fleeting. Quadrant II consists of quieter positive moments—perhaps an early morning in the office before everyone else gets in. What is it that brings you what the Eagles called a "peaceful, easy feeling"? What takes you to your "happy place"? Whatever ritual or location or person takes you there, you're in quadrant II when you feel the ease and simple enjoyment of existence.

Following are some of the drivers of increases in oxytocin, norepinephrine, and dopamine, and therefore of increases in quadrant I and II feelings:

Oxytocin: Bonding
- Laughter
- Love/liking/trust
- Collaboration
- Generosity

Norepinephrine: Focus and excitement
- Engagement
- Interest
- Novelty

Dopamine: Completion
- Goal achievement
- Mastery
- Winning

You can download this list from my website at *www.CompleteIntelligence.com* and post it in your office or at home. Keeping that list where you'll see it regularly will help you add a little of each of these positive "primary colors" to your palette each day. In addition, there are five easy, physical things you can do today to bump up your positive chemistry, improve your well-being, and lower your stressor hormone levels, as well as to improve your overall brain function. Try one or more of these when you find yourself lapsing into the negative quadrants:

- Sleep
- Mindfulness or awake rest
- Exercise
- Laughter
- Experiencing significance through connectedness

Of course, if you're feeling overly stressed or depressed, seek the advice of a physician, but the five activities above have been shown to help. They don't require pills or potions, and only one requires the presence of another person.

Because they are so crucial, each will be discussed in depth later in parts III (on stamina) and IV (significance) of this book.

Today, we understand that good and bad feelings are real and have a chemical basis. Some of them warm us, bewitch us, protect us, warn us, and can sometimes hurt us if they keep happening in the negative realm over the long haul. Moment by moment, our neurochemistry is modulating to our perception of events as they are happening. Once you're able to determine approximately which of the four quadrants you're operating in at a given moment, you can make decisions and feel some degree of control over the feelings you're experiencing. How do you know which quadrant you're in? Simply check in with yourself: Do you feel good or bad, anxious or peaceful, frazzled or energized? Then ask yourself whether the feeling is intense or not. Once you get better at answering these questions, you'll be able to figure out your position on the chart and make choices that move you toward the left side.

Many of the triggers—the perceived threats and rewards—we experience come from our environment, especially our interactions with others. In the next chapter, we'll continue to explore how to move from threat to thrive by navigating these triggers.

ACTIVATION

- Reflect on how you feel right now. Are you feeling more positive or negative? Is the feeling intense, or are you in a lower arousal state?

- What can you do to increase your energy or decrease negative feelings?

- When you want to change your state of mind, go back up to the lists of items that induce positive neurochemical reactions and consider how many you're doing regularly—like laughing, trying new things (novelty), and achieving goals.

CHAPTER 3

Moving from Threat to Thrive

IN NEARLY EVERY SITUATION in life, you're moving toward something or you're moving away from something. For instance, do you go to work because you like what you do, or do you go because you don't want to go broke? These are entirely different reasons to go to work, and each can produce a very different neurochemical reaction. The first—you're going to work because you like it—capitalizes on your reward chemistry and the ensuing neural activation. The second—you go because of the paycheck—is an avoidance behavior and is associated with negative feelings: *Wow, this is a drag* or *I really hate being here—I can't wait for Friday.*

Kurt Lewin began writing about this phenomenon some seventy-five years ago,[1] describing it as "approach-avoidance" behavior—our tendency to move toward or away from situations. Since then, many psychologists and neuroscientists studied behavior and brain scans (an fMRI, which is a way to look at blood flow in the brain, which correlates with the underlying brain activity of a person who is actively doing or thinking something) to see approach-avoidance at work. A few scientists went so far as to suspect that approach-avoidance "characterizes most, if not all, of a person's life decisions."[2] Whether that's true or not continues to be debated; some say that arousal and mood have a lot to do with decision making, too. One thing seems clear, however: Approach and avoidance are the ping-pong paddles that bounce us between positive and negative neurochemical states. All the while, our brain is seeking a "safe" place.

Unfortunately, many of us spend a good deal of life in avoidance—the state where we're moving away from something. Think about all the things you do because you want to avoid the perceived negative consequences if you don't. If your list is long, you're not alone. The constant pinging of anxiety can be hard on our body and brain. But if we can shift to an approach state—one where we're moving toward a reward rather than away from a threat—we will likely feel better and get more done. In order to get ourselves into that approach state more often, it's essential to understand the states of mind and social interactions that might put us in an avoidance state.

We can't always choose whether we're in approach or avoidance. If you suffer an intense scare or get an undue insult from the boss, that external event is going to put you into an avoidance state. In times like these, we have to work very hard to choose a more productive, approach-oriented mindset. The brain operates very differently when we feel safe, when we're approaching, than it does when we feel threatened and are avoiding. If we understand the factors that researchers have found can lead to the threatened avoidance state, we're better able to transition to the more productive mindset. I know I like myself best when I'm in a safe state, motivated by moving toward something. Getting there begins with looking at your default approach to the world: Do you lean toward approach or avoidance thinking?

CHANGING OUR PERSPECTIVE, CHANGING OUR NEUROCHEMISTRY

Reframing the reason we do something can change our relationship with the situation and even the neurochemistry that's triggered in response to it. I began working with my personal trainer, Tony, because I wanted to *avoid* gaining more weight. I had been showing friends vacation pictures when we came across one of me in my swimsuit. I exclaimed that I had man boobs—and no one disagreed. Not even a polite attempt to lie! That did it for me. I knew I needed to lose some weight, so I went to Tony to do just that. However, I knew after only a few weeks of working out that I was framing my workouts as avoidance, and it made trips to the gym a total chore. It was a constant struggle, and I felt bad.

But eventually, I managed to change my motivation for working out with Tony. I'd been studying the brain, and I became convinced that the single best thing we can do for our brain is exercise. After having that realization,[3, 4] I was no longer moving away from the threat of being overweight; I now frame exercise as moving toward having a healthier brain and, consequently, a healthier body. Every time Tony puts me through a nasty little torture, I just think about the positive chain of chemical and vascular happiness going on in my body. That's a different feeling than begrudgingly working out—more quadrant II than quadrant III.

From time to time, stop and ask yourself how you're living your life: Are you doing what you do to avoid losing something, or are you doing it because it feels good and gives you a sense of well-being? What is the biggest thing you are avoiding right now? How could you reframe it to make it feel like you're approaching, not avoiding? Be careful not to use avoidance language in your reframing; some avoidance behaviors can masquerade as approach behaviors. Consider the work example. If you dread your job and get nothing out of it besides the money, you could tell yourself that you're moving toward your monthly paycheck when, really, you're in an avoidance mindset: You only want that paycheck to avoid hunger and the bill collector. A true approach mindset might see you motivated to go to work because you want to get so good at what you do that you'll have an even more rewarding career than the one you have. It's not always as simple as that, but being aware of how we approach our everyday lives can help us control how we feel and behave.

SEEKING SAFETY IN OUR SOCIAL INTERACTIONS

One of the best ways to evaluate whether you're in approach or avoid mode is to note how you feel and act when you're around other people. In every encounter you have, your brain is categorizing the interaction—several times per second without our knowing—as either a reward or a threat.[3, 4] We then behave accordingly, moving toward reward and defending against or moving away from threat. All day long, in just about every encounter I have with others, especially when the encounter has a negative aspect, I stop to evaluate whether I'm feeling threatened or whether I'm pursuing something worthwhile in the interaction. Try doing the same in your daily interactions. Check in with how you feel—good or bad, whether intensely or slightly.

Many psychologists and neuroscientists have studied approach-avoidance theory and how it affects social equilibrium. Earlier, I mentioned Kurt Lewin as a progenitor of the approach-avoidance idea, and many have followed in his wake. In his book *Drive*, author Daniel Pink writes about the approach-avoidance idea as it relates to autonomy, mastery, and purpose. Martin Seligman gives his take on living in an approach mindset in his book *Flourish: A Visionary New Understanding of Happiness and Wellbeing*. In an earlier and acclaimed book, *Learned Optimism*, Seligman shows how avoidance or pessimism can lead to depression, while reframing in a more approach-based style leads to better overall mental health and helps to ward off some depression.

David Rock, author of *Your Brain at Work*, offers a particularly helpful way to think about approach and avoidance with his SCARF model.[5] Rock's model offers up a quick way to think about whether we're feeling safe or threatened in social situations—whether we're moving away or toward. The letters in SCARF stand for *status, certainty, autonomy, relatedness,* and *fairness,* and research tells us that threat or reward states are initiated when there is a lack or abundance of one or more of these areas. When we understand these five areas and can analyze how they play into our own lives, we're better equipped to consciously transition from avoiding to approaching—and from survive to thrive. To that end, let's take a closer look at each element of the SCARF model.

Status: Where Do We Fit in the Pecking Order?

Status is about where we stand in relation to other people. Do we have the highest title in the room, or the lowest? It makes a difference in how we interact with the people around us. Those with higher status tend to feel safer, while those with lower status are more likely to be in a threatened state. Of course, your status isn't fixed; it can even change many times throughout the day. Think about your status at work, and at home, and in the community. Our sense of authority changes with status and our neurochemistry follows, initiating emotions associated mostly with quadrant II when we have a higher status and quadrant III when we have a lower status. To see how status changes our behavior, think about how you are when you're interacting with your boss's boss—probably more guarded and polite than usual. The sense of slight threat narrows your behavior a bit. Now think of yourself when you're interacting with peers or with employees who report to you. Are you looser, maybe more jovial, bossier? Status can present a threat when we don't have it and a reward when we have the opportunity to get more of it.

ACTIVATION

- Status: If you're the boss, give status to a direct report by telling them they are the lead on a certain project and that you will respect their decisions. Also, refrain from needing to always be the smartest person in the room. Give others the chance—even if you know the answer.

Certainty: Our Brains Crave Knowing What's Next

The second element of the SCARF model is certainty. Certainty gives us a sense of control, and we're wired to want it, if not crave it. When our ancestors awoke each day and stepped outside their dwellings, they wanted to be certain of what dangers lurked around the corner, so they were on high alert. Not knowing what was out there could lead to their death. Thanks to the hypervigilance of our amygdalae on surprises in the environment, we continue to have that same need.[6] Since the brain is a linear processing machine, it's looking for patterns, and certainty in those patterns, in order to make sense of the world.

When we have certainty, we feel safe. Uncertainty, however, makes us want to only do what feels safe, which means we fall back to tried-and-true behaviors while shunning anything that's innovative or daring. The need for too much certainty can cause paralysis and a lack of spontaneity. Look at Wall Street: The financial sector's need for certainty each quarter can cripple companies looking to create and execute long-term strategies that don't provide a lot of certainty.

If you're in an organization going through massive change, you're going through an exercise in uncertainty. Employees become protective and have a tendency to do what they've always done because the predictable results feel safe. Every organization is changing all the time—some more than others because of mergers, acquisitions, and staff resizing. That's scary. The paradox is that at these precise times, we typically want new thinking, intelligent risk-taking, and competent decision making—but these things are more difficult in an uncertain environment.

When you start feeling uncertain because one aspect of your life is about to change, it's a good idea to find comfort in a routine that's not going to change. It can be something as simple as working out or beginning the workday by organizing your office. It gives your brain a break from the threat state of uncertainty and may help you shift out of the avoidance state in the other areas of your life.

ACTIVATION

- Certainty: Use agendas for meetings and stick to them. Communicate what is *not* going to change when things are changing rapidly. Create weekly rituals with your team (open the Monday meeting with what great things happened over the weekend). Conversely, override the need for certainty and sometimes go into the scary unknown. Life becomes more interesting when it's sometimes spontaneous.

Autonomy: The Power of Choice

Jeff Immelt, chairman and CEO of GE, was once asked what he thought was a critical leadership attribute. "Decision making," he answered decisively. "The ability to make and execute decisions quickly, and then to change course if that's necessary, is going to determine a lot about who leaders are going forward." Immelt feels that choosing a path and then dealing with consequences good or bad is crucial to great leadership.

The good news is that, most of the time, the brain wants to decide. At the very least, making a decision resolves the discomfort that comes when we need to make a choice but haven't yet. Rock calls this desire to make decisions "autonomy"—regulating the self. When we feel like we don't get to make choices we *should* get to make, our amygdalae sound the alarm, and we start feeling threatened. The internal response we might be thinking is often along the lines of "You're not the boss of me! I'll do what I want!"

So, it's interesting that, as Immelt points out, we need to become good at choosing a path—that we want to have choices, and that, ironically, we see many leaders who lack the ability to take decisive action. This tension might have to do with the fact that we're also pulled toward the need to be right—that need to have status, to be the smartest person in the room. Herein lies the push-pull match we play internally every day. If you're aware of that tug-of-war—the desire to decide on one hand, and the desire to not make the wrong decision on the other—you have a better chance of resolving it. They're two sides of the approach-avoid coin, and, as Immelt implies, we're usually better off here, as elsewhere, when we're approaching, not avoiding.

ACTIVATION

- Autonomy: Avoid prescribing *the* path someone should take, but rather describe the options available and let them make the decision between a set of acceptable choices.

Relatedness: Fitting In with More Than Kin

Since we were little ones, we've all wanted to fit in with a group. There are few things that feel better than being welcomed into a group and feeling a sense of belonging. Of course, the need for belonging has a good and bad side.

One of the most heartbreaking but early learned punishments we experience is banishment from the group. It happened on the playground and it can happen in the workplace. When our ancestors used banishment from the clan as a punishment, they were essentially sentencing someone to death because of the dangerous world beyond the clan. Alone, the banished person met with the treachery of harsh climates, killer animals and plants, and the difficulty of gathering food. Alone, we are too weak, but together we become strong enough to survive all of these things.

Still today, the feeling of being related is an enormous psychosociological pull. We are so sensitive to social rejection and ostracism that they actually activate the same pain receptors in the brain as when you break a bone.[7] We survived by being in the tribe, not outside it. Today, the "in group" is the popular one; the "out group" is not. Think about when you thought you should be included in a meeting or conversation and you weren't. It feels bad—it's a threat, and you want to move away from it.

ACTIVATION

- Relatedness: Create good ground rules of engagement for your team (meeting lengths, tardiness, casual-dress days, and so on). People want to know how to fit in; give them direction on how they can. Be accessible as a colleague (with parameters!).

Fairness: One of the Brain's Great Rewards

Today, neuroscientists are devoting a lot of their experimentation time to the concept of fairness. They've discovered a place in the brain that responds to fairness in the same way the brain responds to sex and chocolate: very positively. In other words, the brain sees fairness as a reward.[8] Carnegie Mellon's Golnaz Tabibnia and her associates found that when things are basically equal between two people, the relationship feels positive. When there is an imbalance, no matter how trivial the opposite party believes it to be, negativity seeps in and fireworks start to ignite—in the form of withheld information, passive-aggressive behavior, and complete rejection of the relationship. That tells you something about the evil cousin of fairness: vengeance. The brain's craving for the reward feelings that fairness can create is strong enough that people will often go out of their way to even up the score when they feel jilted.

ACTIVATION

- Fairness: Give everyone the same opportunity to have a shot at major things like jobs, projects, or great work trips. If something feels unfair to you, acknowledge it and communicate it. Often, others have no idea when specific things are important to us; the only way they can is to hear them. Also, mete out rewards, awards, and bonuses based on clear guidelines (especially if you're a boss).

Obviously, this discussion skims the surface of the inner workings of the brain as they pertain to our behavior, but when we come from a place of knowing, we can be more in control of our destiny—living by design, not by default. The neurochemistry of our brain may seem like an arcane set of fluids and electrical transmissions that are difficult to visualize. But we can see them acting out in our social selves every single day, at every moment. Once you're aware of them, you'll see them play out in nearly every aspect of our business and personal lives. I wish it was as easy as going to the paint store and mixing a little of this and a little of that to come up with the exact perfect amount of neurochemistry for the moment. It's not, of course. Our gift is our greatest challenge—our ability to think about things in the past and in the future and assign emotional states to them. Those states, as you've discovered, drive our behavior and can be productive and sometimes destructive.

Now that we've laid that foundation, we can move on to the rest of the book, where we'll see how you can increase your sense of control over your life, improve your stamina, and increase your feelings of significance.

2

Controlling Your Success

CHAPTER 4

Taking Control of Your Life

THERE'S A SHOPPING MALL near my house with an indoor playground for kids. I find it fascinating to watch the joy, the lunacy, and—unfortunately—the inevitable tears that come with kids in a play state. There are enormous adult lessons in children's play, and watching them is an amazing way to understand how adult humans wrestle with the issue of control. We're all just big kids at heart; the content of our games is simply different and more sophisticated.

Kids display their struggles with control a little more readily, while adults learn to hide and mask it. Still, as adults, if we don't possess enough control, the emotional center of the brain can get out of hand. Think of the emotional center of the brain as a playground filled with two- to six-year-olds, all screaming and running all over the place in their own particular way. Without some adult supervision, things can quickly get out of control. The prefrontal cortex, as we learned in chapter 1, helps us stop and reason before we act on our emotions; it's the supervisor to the limbic system—the emotional center symbolized by all those kids. We bring control to our emotions in part because we want to avoid being disciplined by the supervisor. We're often rewarded for controlling ourselves by an increased sense of well-being. Plus, we are often rewarded—in our jobs, at home, in our communities—when we show that we can make good decisions, be confident, exert willpower, and achieve goals—all part of our control mechanisms.

The idea of feeling in control has been a central focus of psychologists and neuroscientists for years, and now we understand even more fully how it affects our work lives.[1] We have learned that the feeling of control is an essential emotional attribute. Ultimately, we want to be in control of where we're going and how we get there (recall David Rock's exploration of autonomy as a key neurosocial driver). We sometimes go so far as to convince ourselves that we can control our emotions so completely as to make decisions or conduct negotiations "without emotion." While being devoid of any emotion is basically impossible for the normal brain, regulation of emotion puts us in the driver's seat—in control—both personally and professionally.

From a day-to-day perspective, control is central to our success. It gives us direction and helps us be self-directed enough to achieve our goals. When we feel safely in control, we can make plans for a direction—our goals—and control also gives us impetus to get started on those goals. It can change just about everything we do, from how we behave in meetings, to how we give and receive performance reviews, to how we negotiate, to how we give high-stakes presentations. When we're in control, we can make ethical choices, hold off on impulsive decisions, listen more appreciatively, perform better in our job, manage the enormous anxiety that often comes from high-pressure jobs, and be more effective overall. Our sense of control also influences things like working memory—the type of surface memory that allows us to be fluid in our thinking from moment to moment, is critical for selective attention so that we can get things done, and is the mainstay of impulse control.

Control is both a biological and a sociological phenomenon—it shows up in the brain's circuitry and chemistry, and it's considered a positive attribute in most social settings. A sense of control brings on the neurochemistry of pleasure. It is a rewarding feeling. And feeling a lack of control can be almost debilitating in life.[2]

To better understand how to leverage control in your life, you must first understand your personal relationship with control. We all have an internal or external focus when it comes to control, and understanding your current perspective will help you move to a more positive position. We'll do that in the following section. Following that, we'll grapple with what happens when we have too much control or become obsessed with control, and you'll learn how to spot warning signs in your own life. Finally, in this chapter's final section, you'll learn a basic skill for moving to a greater sense of control in your life—defining your own success.

CONTROL IS ABOUT PERSPECTIVE: EXTERNAL VERSUS INTERNAL CONTROL

Who is responsible for your success? Is it your broker, your life partner, your parents, your boss, your employees—all of whom can hand us opportunities or throw us curveballs? Or is your success in your hands and your hands alone? These are two very different ways of framing who has control over our success in life, and which one we lean toward can have a large impact on our lives.

Psychologists refer to this as an external locus of control (others have control) versus an internal locus of control (you have control). Most of us have a mix of the two, but when confronted with a certain situation, many of us will default to one of these two attitudes. Let's say you don't get a job promotion because one of the requirements is that you have an MBA. If you're internally focused, you'll likely investigate how to get an MBA and take the steps toward that or make a decision to go on a job path that doesn't require one. You see yourself as having control over that situation, and you're able to be proactive. If you're externally focused, however, you might blame the inflexibility of the interviewer or the rules of the company on the lack of an offer. You'd be less likely to take the steps toward getting an MBA because you would see it as someone else's problem, not yours.

Think about where you fall on the spectrum—are you closer to the internal or external side? Both extremes have their upsides and downsides. If you have a strong internal sense of control, you will likely be more self-directed and goal oriented, but you might also suffer from blaming yourself for events that are indeed out of your control. I met a corporate VP in one of my classes who had an intense internal locus of control. Responsibility oozed out of her mouth every time she spoke. During a break, she confided in me that she just discovered that she had cancer and that she should have seen it coming. It was her fault, she believed, that the disease had gotten as far as it had. That deep internal focus is filled with all kinds of self-blame and other unproductive emotions. On the other hand, if you are externally focused, you may blame circumstances or other people for failures in your life, losing sight of the control you do have over the path your life takes.

Although both sides have their drawbacks, throughout this book, I'll be nudging you toward an internal focus. When you feel that sense of control over what happens to you, you're more likely to be successful. You'll take responsibility for the ups and the downs that come your way—a not-so-secret secret to success. Being aware of what we can control puts us in the driver's seat. You can start moving toward an internal locus of control by simply listening to the way you speak. When something occurs that isn't to your liking, if your immediate response is to look for all the reasons why others or circumstances caused this bad thing in your life, take a moment before responding and reframe the statement into an "I" statement. What did you have to do with the scenario? What could you have done to change the outcome? That's taking control. When we switch our language, we open up our brain to the possibility of learning from the mistake. Conversely, when we blame others, they are the ones who have to learn before the outcome can change—and how could we possibly control that?

In a 2014 interview, a major star in the National Football League criticized the press for its coverage of his outburst about an opposing player after a big divisional championship game on national TV with thirty million people watching. He was endlessly interviewed for several days after the incident. He apologized for his nasty comments and explained that the intensity of competition brings out a different side of him. It was admirable that he was taking responsibility for his humanity. But when the interviewer asked him if he had any regret about the comments, something shifted. He said that he regretted how the media had taken the comment and blown it up so large that it took the focus off his teammates and their great win.

"What's wrong with that comment?" you might ask. "Maybe the media did overblow it." Perhaps, but this player went from taking responsibility for his actions to blaming TV reporters for what they do—create sensational television. In essence, his second comment said that his team was suffering because of the media attention, not because of him and his televised outburst. It is difficult to completely own our foibles without saying, "Yes, I did that, but . . ." and then going on to explain why we should be excused. Still, it would have been more elegant for this star player to stop before he got to the blame. We all have moments that are not exactly perfect, but owning them is more attractive than blaming them on someone else.

Renowned poet and author David Whyte said at an international symposium on emotional intelligence that "we're most loved for our vulnerabilities and our honesty about them." Even though we want to disown our foibles, we may actually hurt ourselves when we do that. Competence, excellence, meeting deadlines, beating budgets, showing consideration, collaborating, and the like are half of who we are. The other half is made up of our shortcomings—being late, the inability to see the big picture in a particular instance, dictatorial moments, bad relationships that indicate a lapse in our emotional intelligence, and so many other situations that show us for the humans we are. As you'll learn in the next chapter, part of control is confidence, which means we accept the entire picture of who we are—both good and bad. Of course, that knowledge doesn't allow us to abdicate responsibility for self-improvement or from ownership of those bad moments.

An excellent way to switch your focus from external to internal is to start noticing examples of these two positions in others, whether in people you work with or stories in the news. You'll hear it in quick retorts: "Jack, you're late for too many meetings," someone says to Jack, and he replies, "I know, but too many people are scheduling meetings with me." Seems like a plausible excuse, but Jack is blaming the environment for something he does in fact have control over. If Jack reframes his position and sees that control lies within him, he might say instead, "I know. I'm going to look at how I schedule meetings, because this doesn't work the way it is right now." The first example acknowledges that the universe is unfair in the amount of meetings it requires of Jack. The second one lays out a corrective action that Jack will take. Once you've become adept at seeing the two loci of control in others, start noticing examples of your own framing.

This next example of this concept is an extreme case, and yet it serves to illustrate how external focus in general can lead to unpleasant outcomes. When I was conducting interviews on death row in 1986, I learned a lot about human nature, both good and bad—and much of it had a control theme to it. I was there to interview death row inmates for a documentary on capital punishment. While at Florida State Prison, word got out of a study going on with one of the inmates who was an identical twin. It was a gene study about whether we have a choice about how our genes are expressed. Many tests were done on this man and his twin brother, who was a successful stockbroker, and both were interviewed about why they believed they had ended up with their particular fates in life. The death row inmate indicated that it was an easy answer: he and his brother grew up with a single father who abused drugs and alcohol, and the abuse didn't stop at the pill or alcohol bottle—it continued on the little boys. He recounted growing up afraid because he and his brother were beaten just about every day. The inmate said that violence was the only way he knew how to survive in the world. It eventually led him to the electric chair in Florida.

When researchers asked the inmate's twin brother why he believed he ended up where he was in life, he gave some of the same details his brother had. But he continued to describe when they finally went to school for the first time. They were deemed too violent to be together in the same school, let alone the same class, and so they were separated. One day, the stockbroker brother explained how he was smashing the face of a kid into the gravel on the playground when his teacher rushed over to stop them. He did what he said he instinctively knew to do anytime an adult came at him with angry eyes. He kicked her as hard as he could, making contact with her shin and causing it to bleed. She swept him up as he kicked and pounded and screamed. She pulled him in tight, essentially creating a straitjacket with her arms around his legs and arms. And then she whispered something in his ear that would change the trajectory of his life: "When we hurt, we don't hit; we hug." And that was precisely what she was showing him how to do at that moment. She told him from that day forward that anytime he felt like hitting somebody while he was at school, he should instead find her and give her a big hug. She helped the boy understand that he had control: he had a choice to make even in the most dire of circumstances. He chose the hug, often.

For our purposes, the important thing about this story is not so much the gene study as it is the light the story sheds on the power of an internal locus of control. By choosing to nurture or ignore the genetic tendencies we're born with, we can have a hand in causing unwanted behavioral expression to go dormant or become extinct, as with the stockbroker, or cause the gene to fully express itself, as with the inmate. Unfortunately for the inmate and for society, his gene expression was hugely negative and completely externally focused. But, ultimately, we can all make a conscious choice to take control of our future and to stop blaming the past, others, and circumstances. When we get stuck in our past, we're essentially saying, "I have no control over my future." But taking control of the future is one of the single greatest gifts we can give ourselves; when we do so, we get to have a say in the outcome of our lives.

THE DOWNSIDE OF CONTROL

As I've mentioned before, control has a dark side. For me, it comes out when I'm riding in a car with someone else driving. In that situation, I have to make an active and conscious effort to give up control. I "just know" that my internal map knows the better way to get to where we're going. When I force myself to let go and allow my prefrontal cortex to get into my mental discussion, I realize it does not matter one iota if we get there fifteen seconds or fifteen minutes later going the direction the driver is going—and we may even arrive earlier. At that moment, I can relax and pay attention to other things, including the amazing company I'm riding with.

An inner control freak lurks in all of us. The freak comes out in different situations for each of us, and it typically happens when there's a lack of trust, when we feel that the other individual's judgment isn't reliable. It's one of the reasons we don't like control freaks; it feels like they don't trust us, and that can be damaging to a relationship. What are the areas in your life where you feel the need to control when it might not serve your purpose? For instance, are you a micromanager who can't let go of managing all the details of your employees' work because you know the best and only way to get something done? If your need for control lurks in backseat driving or needing the perfectly clean office or your desire to always get a word in on every subject, warn others when you're going into that situation. When we're aware enough to know and to take responsibility for our overly controlling impulses, we get a lot more forgiveness for these rough edges.

Giving up control is a kind of control in itself. It means learning to control the impulse we feel to speak up or jump in. That is harder than it sounds. One tactic is to have a quick internal conversation and ask yourself whether the person on the receiving end of your control is grateful for your intrusion. Also evaluate your trust level with the other individual. If you don't trust them, there is work to be done in the relationship so that they can feel less controlled and you can be less controlling. (You'll learn how to improve relationships like this when we get to chapter 13, about connectedness and trust.)

Part of feeling in control without trying to exert undue control over others is understanding what appropriate control can bring us—namely, success. And those who craft their own definition of success are more able to feel in control—which enables them to direct their efforts toward achieving goals, a trait of successful individuals. It's a circular construction. Let's now look at how to define success.

DEFINE SUCCESS TO ACTIVATE CONTROL

When we define and understand what success is for us, the likelihood that we can feel more in control increases. One of my favorite parables about how success means something different to each of us is about a simple fisherman who meets a businessman.[3] The fisherman explains his modest life of fishing; napping with his wife; playing with his grandchildren; and meeting his friends for music, food, and fun each night. The businessman is incredulous that the fisherman hasn't strategically thought about expanding his business into fleets of fishing boats and creating multimillions in profits. The fisherman asks the businessman how long this will take and what the result will be. The businessman tells him that, after he has spent 20 years or so making his fortune, the fisherman will then be able to go fishing; nap with his wife; play with his grandchildren; and meet his friends for music, food, and fun each evening.

Whether it's a simple catch each day or running a megaconglomerate, defining what success means is one of the keys to control. In chapter 7, on goal

achievement, we will address how to refine your goals and how achieving those goals will create positive "success messages" in your brain. For now, consider what the big picture of success looks like for you.

ACTIVATION

- Write down your definition of success. What would make a successful year, month, day in your life? The more specific you can be, the better.

- For an added twist and a great discussion, ask your significant other to do the same thing separately and then swap what you've written. Compare answers. One of my closest friends and his wife do this every year, and he says it makes them feel closer and more aligned about success in their lives—and that it's simply fun to do.

The upside of well-placed control is one of the most prized human attributes: the feeling of confidence. That's next.

CHAPTER 5

The Confidence That Comes With Control

THE MEGAHIT TELEVISION PROGRAMS *Survivor*, *The Apprentice*, and *The Voice* all have one thing in common—British producer Mark Burnett. In an interview about how he became arguably the most successful producer of American television of all time, he said, "First, I've always done things I was interested in, but I don't think anyone can ever tell you that they know if anything is really going to work for sure. But, you do it anyway. We all know that those who need to be 100 percent sure of something never do anything." Burnett's insightful comment is the central tenet of confidence: the willingness to jump into something without a 100 percent guarantee. Since few things in life, if any, offer that kind of guarantee, we have to have confidence to get things done, feel good about our accomplishments, and be willing to try new things—all of which are good for us and our brains. Most of us would like more confidence; it consistently shows up on lists of the most admirable traits.

How do we get more confidence? Well, one thing that seems constant in the theories and research is that we have confidence when we feel we have some sense of control over a particular circumstance or outcome—we may not be certain how it will turn out, but we have at least a kernel of control over what happens.

My fitness trainer, Tony, recently had mouth surgery. His teeth are all sorts of difficult for him. His baby teeth haven't completely fallen out, and some of his adult teeth are waiting to emerge, but many are apparently too big for his mouth. He got new braces before the surgery so that the new adult teeth aren't destructive to his mouth when they do come in. His smile is filled with widely spaced teeth. I've known Tony for four years. I've only noticed his teeth a few times, but he always smiles—even when he is battering my body, especially then. Tony has strong self-confidence, and we all see him as an assured, fun-loving, ever-smiling cool guy. If he were busy covering up his teeth, we would likely notice that instead of his infectious smile. Tony exudes confidence, so that's what we notice. Tony was aware of his teeth, of course, but he did something confident people do—he took control of the situation, and when he could afford to do something about it, he did. Until then, his teeth were just a part of his charm. Confidence is not about perfection. As Mark Burnett so aptly suggested, we won't ever get off the couch if we wait for perfection.

Confidence is also part of a virtuous circle—when we have it, it's easier to get more of it. Without confidence, however, we might not have the courage to get some in the first place. Acquiring confidence requires a dash of daring and belief in ourselves. We have to avoid confidence killers, like comparisons; we have to rely on our strengths and times of success to build trust that we can be successful again; and we have to try new things to practice our confidence. Because like most things, building your confidence can become a habit if you work at it.

SELF-CONFIDENCE, COMPETENCE, AND BELIEF IN OURSELVES

Andrew stands beyond the point of no return on a double-black-diamond ski run that our mutual friend, expert skier Ed, has led him to at Loveland Basin in Colorado. He later told us how furious he was at first: This ski run is nearly straight down, with some "little ledges" of rocks (Ed's description). This is well beyond the scope of Andrew's skiing ability. Then Andrew blows off his anger and musters his courage. The only way down is, well, down—even if he snow-plows the entire thing or takes it down on his butt. He eventually made it to the bottom of the run with huge zigzags down the mountain. Andrew took so long to get down to the bottom, where we were waiting, that it shaved thirty minutes off our ski day.

Andrew is generally a confident man. He knows his abilities, and had he been asked, he likely would have opted out of a ski run so clearly beyond his ability. But he wasn't asked. And isn't that how it is many times? We are asked to do something in our job that is not to our liking and may be beyond our skill level. That's when belief in ourselves is essential. Do you believe, in general, that "you can"? There is no easy way to get that "I can" attitude, but it appears that those who practice *not* being 100 percent certain before taking the plunge are better at mustering the courage and confidence to act. The perfectionists in the crowd suffer from a lack of self-confidence more often because that 100 percent mark is so elusive.

In talking about it later, Andrew admitted that gathering the courage to make it down the hill, instead of trudging several yards back uphill, was not about him imagining that he would or should look like an Olympic-caliber skier. He said he did not once consider comparing himself to the expert skiers flying by as he struggled to stay upright. Andrew says it was about telling himself that somehow he could make it to the bottom in one piece. His belief got him started.

A big chunk of self-confidence is courage, and another is our belief in our ability to do something, overall, and that belief helps predict how we will interact with the future. Your belief in your own ability to accomplish your goals is called self-efficacy. If your goal is to be a good presenter, and you believe you will be, with some guidance and practice, then you're more likely to do what it takes to get there. The Centre for Confidence and Well-Being in the United Kingdom says confidence is self-efficacy plus optimism.[1] Optimism is, of course, your positive feelings and hope about the future; it's not about having an overly rosy view of the future but about believing you can do what you need and want to do.

Self-confidence is not necessarily a fixed trait. It's something that can come and go with our ability level. Yet those who are generally self-confident usually try more things, even when they lack any ability. Their belief ignites their courage to try. Those with low self-confidence will often tell themselves they can't do something well, so they won't try at all. Andrew was confident that he would get to the bottom of the mountain; how and when were not the issue. He did not have a high level of skill, but he believed he could solve the problem of getting down.

So, confidence isn't automatically equated with skill, even though we often act as if it is. While it can appear that only masterful people are confident, we don't always see the times they attempted something and failed. I have seen extremely confident people fail miserably at an activity and keep their self-confidence intact. They feel good about themselves in general, and they feel good that they even tried. Of course, self-confident individuals feel somewhat bad when they miss their target, but they're more resilient and bounce back more quickly than those who lack a general sense of self-confidence.

Confident people try new things without comparing themselves to others. They might use another person's skill as a benchmark or an example, but they don't compare themselves with that person to lay out a pecking order. Instead, they compare to learn. Confident individuals are focused on the experience and the feedback they get from those who can do better than them. They may even ask those better than them for direct and constant feedback so that they have a chance to improve their competence. I was describing this concept to an executive, and he told me that his boss does this well. The boss deemed this guy to be a great presenter, so every time the boss gives a presentation, he asks the executive to give him one thing he can improve the next time—and "You were fine" isn't an option. This boss has enough self-confidence to solicit feedback from his employee because he knows that he himself doesn't have the skill level he wants to achieve eventually. It's another example of how self-confidence is a circular concept: You get more of it when you try something and then succeed, and you need it in order to even attempt in the first place.

Even those with high competence or even mastery in a skill might struggle with confidence. Recently, at a medical conference, I witnessed one of the most competent people in his field completely stumble in his presentation before an audience of several hundred other physicians. He was an undisputed master in his subject area, but on the day of the presentation, he seemed to lack the confidence to deliver his knowledge to a thousand eyeballs staring back at him. He may have been suffering from perceived high expectations and the feeling that he needed to be perfect in front of his peers; that may have put his focus on himself and how he looked instead of on the audience and what they would learn.

Perfectionism is just one of the confidence killers that many of us fall victim to in our careers and life. Let's look at it and a couple others.

THE CONFIDENCE KILLERS: PERFECTIONISM, COMPARISON, AND WHAT-IFS

Corporate halls are filled with high-ranking businesspeople who have difficulty acknowledging their level of mastery; they're always striving for the unattainable perfection that pulls them forward. Once we achieve a certain level of mastery, it is difficult to admit to ourselves that we have accomplished a great thing. The mantra is to always do more, be more, and have more. That is fine. Striving is an important part of excellence. However, so is humbly accepting that we have achieved a level of excellence already. It doesn't mean we stop striving. It means we can be compassionate with ourselves in a way that fills our confidence bucket—not our arrogance bucket. If we don't get off the ride on the way to the mysterious place of perfection and take stock, we are certain to become the exact person we don't want to be. Feeling like a failure can put us in a foul mood. We become barking tyrants who create in the lives of employees, colleagues, and others around us the misery we feel in ourselves for not always hitting the mark. If you have perfectionism coursing through your veins, beware. In its extreme form, perfectionism is considered an anxiety disorder. It's a driver and a confidence killer at the same time.

Let's go back to skiing to uncover our next confidence killer: comparing ourselves to others. Say you've never tried skiing before. You'll probably fall a lot when you first get on skis, but with a few basic lessons, you can turn and stop. Do you decide never to ski because you lack the ability to do it well? If so, you're limiting yourself to only the things you already know how to do. For those people with an external locus of control, new skills are difficult, because their tendency is to blame the environment for any less-than-perfect performance. Those who lack self-confidence and who are unwilling to take control of the environment are doomed to self-comparison and blame when they constantly compare themselves to others who can do something better than them. Comparing ourselves to others is tricky because we naturally do it, but if it stops us from adventuring out to try new things, the only person who loses is us.

Successful people take control and take the steps necessary to at least make it down the mountain. Certainly, the feeling of self-confidence may go up when we get better at something, but resist believing that confidence will always follow from competence. When asked what makes them feel self-confident when they are presenting, most presenters will say they feel confident when they "know their stuff." But remember the physician a few pages ago. Think about other brilliant PhD scientists or engineers who "know their stuff" and completely flop as a presenter. Their knowledge does not give them self-confidence. So what is it? They are likely focused on comparing themselves to others.

Their less-than-riveting performance may be weighed down by a little voice that whispers to them that great presenters don't sweat or feel anxiety before they speak. Rubbish. All rubbish. The self-confident individual in this situation says, "I know my topic; it's a normal physiological phenomenon to get a little anxious before presenting; it's actually a signal that I am alert; it's okay to sweat in front of others—no one ever died doing it. Just go." For some people, though, it is difficult to assume this mindset.

Our worries about performance, our comparisons to others, and our lack of confidence often lead to a third confidence killer: "what if" thinking, which can wreak even more havoc on our confidence. It's a vicious cycle and it takes focus and attention to break out of it. For some people, it requires daily work. Here's a method to calm the "what if" jitters that has practical application in other areas of self-confidence. See if you can apply it to your own situation when your confidence is hampered by worry over what could go wrong.

ACTIVATION

- Visualize the worst possible scenarios that could happen in situations that give you a crisis of confidence. For our presentation example above, the list might look like the following: PowerPoint failure, microphone doesn't work, you forget an important piece of your presentation, an executive interrupts your flow and wants to skip ahead to the middle of your slides, someone hijacks the presentation by going on and on about their own experience, someone challenges your data and the credibility of it, and any other nightmare you can think of that could realistically happen.

- Assess the percentage of the likelihood of each scenario happening from 1 to 100. It is often realistically much lower than our fear-laden brain is magnifying it to be.

- Now visualize what you would do in each scenario to recover. No detail is too small to think about. Your brain wants a plan. Give it one. You might even practice your plan by saying certain phrases out loud, by going through physical motions.

In this confidence-building activation, you see that this simple formula works to bring some certainty to the threat architecture in our brain and helps us access the executive, reasoning center of our brain. As you'll learn later in the chapter, when we give our brain a pattern to rely on, we can leverage that pattern in high-stress situations. That's precisely what we do when we visualize realistic worst-case scenarios and then plan what to do if they happen: We give our brain a pattern to go through should that eventuality arise.

Of course, perfectionism, comparisons, and what-ifs aren't the only confidence killers that creep into our day and spoil our belief in ourselves, but they are some of the biggest. Take a moment now and think about which confidence-killing situations you're likely to encounter. Is it a performance review with your boss where you anticipate negative feedback? A meeting with a client from a large account? Maybe the chief executive from your company is coming and you'll have an audience with her. Maybe you're meeting a possible life partner on a blind date. As you can see, the list of things that can cause that fiddly anxious feeling and displace our confidence is seemingly endless.

Try the activation above, apply it to your crisis of confidence, and see how it works for you. The entire activation is about control—mostly controlling what *might* come up in the future. Remember, our brain deplores uncertainty about the future and calms down when we have a good idea of what is next.

Over time, we can learn to trust ourselves to the point where we become comfortable with the discomfort of the unknown—and that can be one avenue to confidence.

Let's now look at two particularly helpful confidence builders you can also put to use next time you feel your confidence slipping away.

CONFIDENCE BUILDER #1: BUILD AND RELY ON YOUR INTUITION

How do you describe how to ride a bike to someone who has never ridden one and get them to ride it perfectly the first time? How do you know exactly which keys to play—without looking—on a piano, in order to play a masterpiece? How do you know a truth from a lie?

It's difficult to verbalize the answers to these questions. We don't have the language for it. We can't explain all of the musculature that goes into the balance of a bike or the proprioception required (the spatial sense of where things are in relation to other things). We also don't have quite the language to tell how we know if someone is lying or not. Our consolidated experiences over a lifetime and tucked into the folds of our brain help us to ascertain quickly how we feel about what someone has just said. It's not a failsafe message from our brain, but it's a piece of data we should not ignore.

When we're called upon to ride a bike or decide between lying and telling the truth, our brain shortcuts right to the relevant information, allowing us to act quickly. Through experience over time we store all the little bits and pieces of information in our brain, and even though we put it in there in fragments, the data is consolidated, and the brain can access it through a remarkable adaptive shortcut. We do a lot of that consolidating as kids (as we learn how to walk and talk and develop eye-hand coordination, etc.). But we continue to do it throughout our lives as we learn and become competent at new things.

If we had to recall all of the elements for a regularly performed motor activity every time we did it, our brain would be overwhelmed and the amount of glucose expenditure would be enormous. We'd be exhausted just brushing our teeth, and we would likely never invent anything new. Our prefrontal cortices would likely be taking naps all day from having to pay attention to so many activities. We've developed a form of instant retrieval so that energy expenditure is less and the load to our brain is minimal.

One such form of instant retrieval is called *heuristics*. That's the word used to describe activities that help us learn through experience and trial and error. It's a form of problem solving and decision making that allows intuition, common sense, experiential learning, and other pieces of information to come together in a matter of a few seconds or less to allow us to make decisions. For the most part, we feel pretty certain and pretty confident when our heuristics kick in and tell us about something; sometimes that information is just that— information—and should be used with other pieces of data to make a well-rounded decision. In his book *Thinking, Fast and Slow*, Nobel Prize winner Daniel Kahneman tells us that the intuitive, heuristic capabilities we have can be highly beneficial in some situations when we have to make snap judgments, while in others, we can be tripped up by not being more deliberate and logical than our biased, intuitive, quick decisions allow.

Your area of mastery or expertise is often a consolidation of skills, experience, and many other small bits of data that add up to a profound knowing. It's been said that it takes approximately ten thousand hours of study to master a topic.[2] That translates to about forty-seven years if we only studied something for an hour every day of the week, except weekends. If we study it four hours daily, we're at more than ten years. Most of us don't have that kind of time to devote to any one thing each day. But our brain picks up on so many things that we don't notice when we're absorbed in a topic. As a matter of fact, study is only one part of heurism. Experience and practice are the others, and it's the consolidation of the three that leads to the sense of intuitive knowing. Over time, that consolidation helps us to know something immediately. Over time, we develop a sense about an activity that allows us to make quick assessments that are often accurate but difficult to explain. Many call it a form of intuition.

Philosopher and biologist Massimo Pigliucci writes in *Answers for Aristotle: How Science and Philosophy Can Lead Us to a More Meaningful Life*, "One of the first things that modern research on intuition has clearly shown is that there is no such thing as an intuitive person *tout court*. Intuition is a domain-specific ability, so that people can be very intuitive about one thing (say, medical practice, or chess playing) and just as clueless as the average person about pretty much everything else. Moreover, intuitions get better with practice—especially with a lot of practice—because at bottom, intuition is about the brain's ability to pick up on certain recurring patterns; the more we are exposed to a particular domain of activity the more familiar we become with the relevant patterns (medical charts, positions of chess pieces), and the more and faster our brains generate heuristic solutions to the problem we happen to be facing within that domain." Heuristics and intuition are some of the most exciting and interesting fields of study today. What is encouraging is that we can all learn heuristically. But if our brain is messy, with too many distractions and overrun with too many things to do, our ability to focus on the environment and pick up heuristic capabilities likely suffers.

Daniel Coyle writes about the idea of getting quiet and going slow to develop talent. Coyle writes in *The Talent Code* that one of the things that highly talented individuals do is something called "deep practice." It's displayed in two facilities he visited that have a high output of "best in the world" performers—one in tennis and the other in classical music. Both places use deep practice as a way to ingrain difficult skills in the neural pathways of the brain. They both have students practice at hyper-slow rates. You might not even recognize the song they are playing or the game they are playing if you were with them; that's how slowly they practice. The idea is to get quiet enough and achieve enough control in the motion that the neural pathway is built impeccably and the action is executed perfectly when brought to real speed. Coyle is describing the ability to consolidate skills in a neural pathway that can be accessed at a moment's notice. Once learned, it happens so quickly that it almost looks like magic to those who do not have the skill. It looks like intuition.

We get better at intuition the more opportunity we have to see and experience things clearly and, according to Coyle's research, slowly. If we're running around with our hair on fire all the time, it's going to be very difficult to sort out feelings, much less make decisions about those feelings. If we get to practice things slowly, in a controlled way and with focus, we eventually get to that heuristic quality. We'll take a closer look at how to build willpower and focus coming up.

Heuristic learning is what helps us become experts on the job as we gather more and more experience and practice. What's the difference between a highly educated college graduate who has learned all of the latest knowledge about finance and an employee who has an additional ten years of experience in finance on top of that college education? Two things: experience and practice, which breed confidence in the latter individual's decision-making abilities. That is valuable to any career, especially in this rapidly moving world.

When we are new in a job, and especially just out of college or a vocational education, we are a lot more transactional in our approach to the job. By transactional, I mean the tasks that you do that are replicable, that another person could do with a little bit of direction. Those transactional skills don't have nearly the perceived value as someone who both knows what to do and is doing it in a flash. The person who knows how and why, and does it without having to think about all the steps, can critically think more quickly and make better decisions overall. That comes from experience and practice.

An executive came up with a great example of the difference between his transactional and heuristic activities. He said scheduling meetings with suppliers in his supply chain is the transactional side, along with getting on an airplane and having those meetings. He can teach anyone how that is done in a short amount of time. The heuristic side is made up of the activities he learned how to excel at after years of trial and error: building deep relationships of trust with vendors, negotiating, and building mutual interest. He explained that he could tell someone the mechanical aspects of those activities but that building trust and learning to read people is just something he knows how to do after years of paying attention to the relationship side of the business. When he walks into those meetings, he is confident that he'll be able to navigate what comes to reach a positive outcome.

There are many examples every day, and it is likely you have your own set of heuristic capabilities. The more you are aware of them, the more you can hone them and articulate your value to others when appropriate.

More importantly, because we are confident when acting within our heuristic capabilities, we can build confidence in other areas by thinking about those activities and how they make us feel. Sometimes, recalling a sense of confidence from another part of our lives or in another situation can help us find the courage to take the necessary actions in our current situation.

ACTIVATION

- What do you do daily that could be adequately explained in a textbook or be taught in a training session? These are your low-value activities that just about anyone could do with relatively little experience. They are the replicable aspects of your job.

- What is it that you are instinctual/intuitive about? What are the things you do in your job that you couldn't easily describe or show to others? These are your heuristic abilities, and you've developed them through practice and experience. They are a sort of wisdom that often appears as a flash of genius.

- Being as specific as possible, write down how you feel when you are relying on your heuristic abilities. What are a few specific moments in which you were successful because of these abilities? Why do you feel the way you do? This will help you build belief in yourself.

CONFIDENCE BUILDER #2: TRY SOMETHING NEW TO PRACTICE CONFIDENCE AND IMPROVE BRAIN HEALTH

Earlier, we said that novelty—doing something brand-new—helps keep the brain engaged. Indeed, doing new things is a powerful tool that can help us grow our brains and grow our confidence. It helps us practice being comfortable with discomfort. Every time we learn something brand-new, we change the shape of our brain, and that new growth actually feels a little uncomfortable as our brain works to make new neural connections. The more we repeat the new activity, the thicker the neural connection becomes and the less effort the brain has to expend in executing the task. It's the old adage "neurons that fire together, wire together." The more your neurons fire together through repetition, the thicker the neural pathway becomes, and soon you've learned a new behavior. This continues throughout your entire life—unless of course you decide to stop learning.

Several years ago, I was invited to dinner in my neighborhood. One of the guests was a seventy-eight-year-old man by the name of John who was as quick and sharp as anyone three times younger. We talked about a variety of topics, and when he found out that I studied and taught facets of human motivation, he asked me what I thought was the single best source of information about motivation. There are plenty of books on motivation, but probably the one that stands out for me in terms of strict motivational research is David McClelland's succinctly titled *Human Motivation*. I saw John about four months later at another neighborhood gathering. He had purchased and read McClelland's dense six-hundred-page tome. He wanted to discuss some theories in it! We chatted, and his probing showed that he really was interested and actually understood the theories very handily. I asked him why he jumped so deeply into the topic, not to mention into this very academic resource on motivation. I will never forget his answer: "Scott, at dinner a few months back, you casually asked me how I kept my mind so sharp, and then dinner conversation from the other end of the table interrupted us. My answer is that I never, ever stop learning. I'm as curious now as I was as a youngster. I'm not done yet." This man is the living lesson of what novelty can do for our brain. Never stop learning. Never. And as John shows us, we don't have to be an expert to enjoy the learning journey. Inspirational, isn't it?

Learning something new can be a yearly goal, an every-few-months goal, or even a daily goal. If it's something bigger like learning an instrument or a language, that is excellent for brain strengthening as an ongoing goal over a year or more. If it is something like learning how to knit or some similar activity, that can suffice as something you do a few times. It's the "struggle" that helps the brain grow. For both our brain and our confidence to benefit, the new learning doesn't have to be something sophisticated, and—this is important and exciting—we don't have to achieve mastery in the new skill or knowledge to benefit from a growing brain.[3, 4] We don't have to become experts; we just have to try and be willing to endure a bit of the discomfort that comes along with growing our brain. Think of the things you've tried, looked ridiculous doing (a form of discomfort), and yet enjoyed thoroughly. Bowling comes to mind for me.

Regardless of any initial embarrassment or discomfort, trying new things grows confidence, and our brains delight more in the first time we do something than any other time, like going to a country we've never been to. There's always a first time for every experience, and the first time is usually one of the most precious to the brain. Sometimes, the positive surprise is the one that comes when we try something new and our brain gives us a self-talk of confidence: "Hey, see? You could do it after all." Have you ever watched someone's eyes after you show them how to do something and they do it? The look is powerful, almost maniacal. It's fueled by the chemistry of joy and confidence. It's a curious thing that on one hand, the brain craves certainty and on the other, it jumps for joy at new experiences.

It's worth repeating that mastery is not the goal. The client services manager in my company, Tami Patzer, took an adult class for organic chemistry. She has absolutely no need for it in the career she is in now. I asked her why she did it. She replied simply, "My daughter is taking it, and we'll be able to help each other with it. The other reason is that I know nothing about organic chemistry. I figured, why not?" She took it, but not for the grade. What she got in return was likely a bigger brain, practice with doing something daring, a new sense of confidence, and time to bond with her daughter over carbons and polymers.

Trying something new requires a dash of daring. I'll quote poet David Whyte again: "Courage is that feeling you get when you're standing on a surface that feels like it can't hold you, but you stand there anyway." Confident people keep going in spite of that little bit of anxiety about what could go wrong. If you feel yourself moving into a threat state as you try a new activity, go back to the activation on page 19 and this time imagine yourself doing the skill or task and think about what you'll do in the eventuality of your worst fear coming to be. Confidence is not competence; it's a willingness to try, and that, in turn, could lead to competence.

ACTIVATION

- Every six months, get on the Internet and research a topic or skill that interests you but in which you have no experience. Start small, but start now, as you look for the steps necessary to begin learning more about that topic or skill. Then go to just one lesson or read one book.

- Do something completely novel once every year or so. Learn to ballroom dance or play the guitar or flute. Learn a new language. Go on a dive trip to the North Pole (yes, there are those kind of dive trips). Learn to fly an airplane or sail a boat. Learn to paint. It's not about mastery. It's about novelty. Keep your brain growing. Start small, but start now. Do something new.

- Go forward with the mindset that it's all right if you look like a beginner. You are. Enjoy the confidence that comes with letting go of having to look like you've already arrived. Don't put any pressure on yourself to be "right" or perfect. Just have fun, enjoy the brain growth, and remember that the more you practice, the better you'll get.

- Think about and write down the thing you like the least about yourself. Why do you dislike this thing? What have others said about it? How has it limited your life or career? Can you do anything to change it? Are you willing to? If not, are you willing to accept this perceived flaw?

- Make a list of the things that you're feeling unconfident about in your job. Visualize, plan, and practice around these situations.

- Reassess your fears. Do you fear these things because they actually happen frequently, or are you just imagining they will?

- Jump. Start now.

Part of feeling confident is feeling that we have willpower to exert in a situation, that we are enough, and even that we have enough. That mindset can help bring us peace and control, and is the next topic for discussion.

CHAPTER 6

Willpower and Focus: Controlling Your Own Attention

WE SPEND A LOT OF OUR brain's energy on self-control or willpower. You may have heard of the famous marshmallow-test studies given to four-years-olds by psychologist Walter Mischel.[1] In the 1960s and '70s, he conducted tests at Stanford University in which researchers tested children's ability to resist eating a marshmallow when they were left alone for fifteen minutes. Some were successful, and others succumbed to the temptation. Look for the studies on YouTube—they will give you a good giggle as child after child works with every fiber of their being to keep from eating the marshmallow.

Mischel followed the children into adulthood and found startling results. In essence, those who had the willpower to keep from eating the marshmallow had higher SAT scores, better body mass indexes, better educational attainment, and other skills later in life than those who didn't wait. Mischel's research shed some light on the importance of learning delayed gratification. It makes sense from both a career and life-skills standpoint. Do I jump at the first promotion offered, even if it doesn't clearly fit my career objectives? Do I buy that furniture on credit now or do I wait and save? One could argue that the easier path leads to trouble more often than the path that requires more patience. But it often takes willpower to make the better decision. It's been discovered that the same limited resource we use in our brain for self-control or willpower is also used in effortful decision making.[2]

Willpower is one of those things we all want and need at points in our life. The abilities to constrain our desires and stay focused are aspects of willpower, and both are inhibitory processes in the brain. This means we have to work hard to stop having our attention pulled to things other than the task at hand or to stick with the choices we make. Willpower keeps us from addictions, keeps us writing the report when those pesky pop-up emails and Facebook notifications want us to do something else, keeps us studying when we want to go play, keeps us on an exercise routine, keeps us saving money instead of spending—and the list goes on and on. It is, in my opinion, one of the single most important skills we have at our disposal, and like all other skills, it takes practice if we want to get better at it.

We can do a few things to strengthen our willpower and ability to focus, each of which we'll cover in the following sections of this chapter. First, we can take control of the distractions in our environment to lessen their impact on us. Second, we can practice willpower, particularly in times when we may have more of it. Third, we can practice being "in the now" to improve our attention. Finally, we can adopt an abundance mindset when it comes to willpower.

MANAGING DISTRACTIONS: THE ULTIMATE IN CONTROL

In the 1970s, researchers went into a school where kids on one side of the school were exposed to frequent train sounds and horns, while kids on the other side of the school were sheltered from the sounds. At the end of a year, they found that students on the train side were one year behind in math aptitude scores.[3] Given this result, imagine what the little nuisances that pop into our day at work do to our work quality. We can all probably relate to that little dog in the animated movie *Up*—he's on a mission but is jolted out of his focus every time he sniffs out and sees a squirrel. He seems like a frantic child saying, "Squirrel! Squirrel!" That's what our distractions are like—shiny pennies (or squirrels) we can't ignore. But to be successful, we must learn to manage them.

How many times has your attention been pulled away while you're reading this book? What about the incoming emails that grab your attention every time they pop up in the corner of your computer screen? (You *can* turn those notifications off.) There are so many things in our environment that scream for our attention. Willpower helps us to tell those things to stand in line. If you are able to focus, you are good at keeping other things from pulling you off your target. It takes willpower to not look at those new emails, the other projects sitting atop your desk, or any other distractions.

Wouldn't it be amazing if we could control all of the distractions that come flying at us each day? The fact is that as long as we're a part of the working world, distractions are probably not going to go away, and could get worse, especially as we accept more responsibility. These distractions can lead to that gnawing feeling of things left undone. The resultant neuro-cocktail can set off a cascade into memory depletion and lost mental acuity. Not so good. As our anxiety goes up, our ability to control our attention goes down. It's a merry-go-round. The more distracted we become, the more difficult it is to manage distractions.[4]

One recent study shows that an interruption of approximately 4.5 seconds triples the amount of errors an individual commits when getting back to the task at hand. An interruption of only 2.8 seconds doubles the error rate.[5] That is huge. If you're engaged in a highly detail-oriented task and you get interrupted, this research shows that you're much more likely to have to go back and correct your work than if you had stayed focused.

Think about the last time you devoted an entire workday to your regular workload. Those days don't come along very often, do they? Most of us are interrupted throughout the day with pleas for help or advice, changed directions on a project, or news that the boss wants something completely different—right *now*. It's as if people are dive-bombing our workspace all throughout the day. We're often left to clean up the mess and get past all the ensuing distractions.

A study done in an IT environment on managing multiple projects in the workplace showed that on average, an individual is interrupted from their work about every three minutes.[6] On average, individuals spent twelve minutes working on a particular work project before a problem arose and took them off in an entirely different direction. Here's the kicker: The study found that we are just as likely to interrupt ourselves as we are to be interrupted by others! We can easily interrupt ourselves with thoughts about things we need to do next week, distracting ourselves from the projects in front of us screaming to be completed. Another finding of this study was that about one-third of the people who were distracted never made it back to the original work project during the day. Finally, about 20 percent of meetings that landed in an individual's day were unscheduled—that is, on top of scheduled meetings and all of the individual's to-dos. By anyone's measures, this is adding up to be an amazing waste of resources, brainpower, and productivity. These statistics only scratch the surface, but they give us a good idea of what we're up against.

Willpower is a finite resource. In laboratories, researchers show that when willpower is tested twice by attempting to interrupt subjects' attention, the second time, they actually do worse on the exact same test.[7] You might think they would get better because they have practice, but the subject's cognitive capacity has been overtaxed, and they can't perform as well on a process that tests focus and the ability to keep on going despite the interruptions.

Consider this: When we crunch all the data—and this is really important—on average, *one hour of focused time is equal to about four hours of distracted time.* In essence, you can get more accomplished in two hours of uninterrupted work than you can in an entire day with the normal distractions. Here's what's even more sobering. When you multitask, you are training your brain to be good at paying attention to distractions. Multitasking is *not* how the brain does its best work. The human brain is a serial processor and, while it's physically possible to do two things at once, it is mentally impossible to give each of the tasks 100 percent of our attention. We are effectively quick-switching between tasks. It's fine to multitask if the two things we're doing don't require real cognitive power and accuracy, like watching TV and putting postage stamps on holiday cards. But the moment one of the tasks does require real brainpower, like doing a detailed spreadsheet, the quality of our output will most likely suffer unless we focus on just one task.

A distracted mind is a messy mind, and a messy mind, compared to one that focuses and stays absorbed in a task, is likely going to be inferior in many measures, including quality of performance, productivity, and anxiety levels, not to mention the memory problems that might occur because we can't get our head wrapped around the task deeply enough. It's like when you read before bedtime and get stuck reading the same paragraph over and over again because you're too tired to focus on it. On those days when we are pulled in many different directions, it's challenging, if not impossible, to keep everything straight. The day becomes one big blur. As our anxiety goes up, we become crankier, and dealing with that cranky, negative-amplifying part of us is difficult and not very good for our reputation or our health if it becomes chronic.

On the flip side, with distractions managed well, we have time to focus and listen to our intuition. We can better build and access our heuristic capabilities, which I described in the previous chapter as a path to greater confidence.

ACTIVATION

- Do *one thing at a time.*

- Turn off pop-up emails and other pop-up notifications that come through your smartphone or computer.

- Consider setting a time when you will check email. I know people who do this, and they have effectively trained colleagues that they look at emails first thing in the morning and then about every sixty to seventy-five minutes thereafter. Others schedule three times a day that they look at and respond to email. Create a system that works for you that manages the constant barrage of dealing with other people's urgencies. If it's urgent enough, your colleagues can call or find you.

- Close your door. Open-door policies sound good, but in practice they can make us less effective by permitting constant interruptions. Schedule appointments rather than letting them pop up whenever someone needs to talk to you. Of course there are the necessary exceptions, but try to distinguish between matters that do need your urgent attention now and those that can wait.

- Work outside your regular workspace (in a coffee shop, library, etc.). For some people, like me, the white noise of a public place increases productivity.

- When you're finished with a file, put it away.

- Do not leave multiple windows open on your computer unless they all have to do with the task at hand.

PRACTICE USING WILLPOWER WHEN YOU HAVE IT

Scores of laboratory tests have shown that our willpower skills become weak if we don't practice them. And even when we are using our willpower regularly, it's a resource that becomes depleted if we don't reenergize through rest and replenish the glucose required for a massive brain process like willpower.

The more tired our brain gets, the more easily distracted it becomes, so it takes even more willpower to stay in the game and remain focused. The later in the day it gets, the more decision fatigue we tend to experience. This happens consistently in the workshops I hold on critical thinking. Early in the day, participants are willing to debate and discuss disparate ideas. Late in the day, they get into rubberstamping and groupthink. In the afternoon, their decisions are much more about getting finished, whereas in the morning, the decisions are more thoroughly debated. Individuals and teams that want to be energized when discussing difficult issues would do well to consider whether their brains are feeling exhausted and, if they are, hold the discussion later.

Roy Baumeister and John Tierney contend in their book *Willpower: Rediscovering the Greatest Human Strength* that the most successful among us are those who are aware of when their willpower is depleted and then take a break when it is. Simple as that. They use their willpower to focus strategically, to stay on task when they have the energy to do so. In practical terms, this might serve you when you're about to be saddled with an intense project with hard-and-fast deadlines. If you're abiding by this awareness theory of willpower, you might decide to work on the project in the morning, when your willpower hasn't yet been heavily taxed, as opposed to working on it when it's been depleted by multiple distractions and decisions later in the day. In this case, you're not exercising willpower per se; instead, you're paying attention to when your willpower is strongest and using it then (and letting it rest once it gets worn out). When we start to become more distracted or irritable, it could be a very good indicator that our willpower is depleted and that it's time to take a break.

Most agree that starting on the most difficult tasks when our brain is freshest is the best strategy. Cognitive overload—the state our brain reaches when we have too much in it—can lead to worse work product. The trick is to get activated to do that thing we don't want to do, but need to do, when our willpower is at its strongest.

In addition to being aware of your energy levels throughout the day and practicing willpower during the peaks, you can also try the other recommendations for practicing willpower in this activation.

ACTIVATION

- Practice doing things differently from how you typically do them. That takes willpower. When I ask workshop participants to change the jewelry or watch from one hand to the other and to keep it there until the next break, 75 percent of them are unable to do this simple task. It takes willpower and practice. Try switching your watch or a piece of jewelry to the other side until the end of this chapter—you'll see!

- Go easy on yourself as you practice. Sticking to a regimen you have never done before is difficult. You're probably going to fall off the horse. Get back on and ride again. You cannot improve your willpower by yelling at yourself.

- Get downtime and rest before you have to jump into a big project that requires your attention. Willpower works best when we are rested.

- Practice saying no to impulses that might not serve you—sleep on them. If you want to buy that fifteenth sweater, it will be there tomorrow after you sleep on the decision.

- Eat. Your brain needs to be loaded with glucose (healthy complex carbohydrates) to exercise willpower—and we get glucose by eating (more on that in the chapter on stamina).

INCREASE YOUR BRAINPOWER BY INTENSELY FOCUSING ON THE PRESENT

In my classes, I use an exercise that I believe can increase brainpower. It follows the adage "be wherever you are." This is, in my estimation, one of the **SINGLE MOST IMPORTANT** concepts of this book. It's about mindfulness—attention training, not relaxation—and it goes to the impact you have in all aspects of your life. Bill George, Harvard professor and former CEO of Medtronic, said, "The main business case for [mindfulness] is that if you're fully present on the job, you will be a more effective leader, you will make better decisions, and you will work better with other people."[8] I'll teach the exercise to you here.

All you need is a raisin and a place to sit. Raisins are good for this exercise because they're strong in flavor and squishy like gum, but you have to concentrate on the raisin if you don't want to swallow it as you're chewing. You could also use a nut, grape, or something else that might be challenging not to swallow after some time in your mouth. The rules for the raisin game are that no one gets to keep time except for me. If you do this alone, set an alarm to go off in ninety seconds. When I say "Go" . . .

> Put the raisin in your mouth for ninety seconds.
>
> During that ninety seconds, you must not swallow the raisin—there must be some remnant of raisin left over when the exercise is finished.
>
> You must also keep the raisin in constant motion; you can't just park it.

The final instruction is that the only thing you can focus on is the raisin itself. Every time you feel your mind wandering, you have to acknowledge it and then get back on the raisin, noticing as much about the raisin as possible.

In this exercise, I am asking you to use your *executive control network* (ECN).[9, 10] This is the network that helps us intensely focus on the present—on being wherever we are. It focuses our mind with only the content we want it filled with. In short, it is mindfulness.

When I have people do the raisin exercise, I look around and notice that nearly every participant has closed their eyes without instruction to do so. The lesson here could be that when we want to intently focus on something, we benefit from limiting the stimulation and distractions in our environment (I'll say it again: Turn off your pop-up emails!). The participants innately manage the distractions in the room by closing their eyes. Being in the present pays off with more than noticing every fold of a raisin, though; it has enormous ramifications for our work output. We can't close our eyes while working on a project, but we can close off many of the things that compete for our attention. It's worth repeating that to give ourselves the best shot at excellent focus, we must minimize the distractions in our environment. Go to an empty office and work, or close the office door. Start to create the brain environment for your best ECN.

Back to class and the ECN raisin exercise: When I ask how long they felt the exercise went on for, about half of the participants say that it feels like it went on for a long time. The other half feels like the time goes by rapidly, possibly because they are so absorbed in the activity.

When I ask participants about what they experienced, they say that it is very difficult to stay focused on the raisin and that they're stunned at how many times their mind wandered in just ninety seconds. This is another lesson about our distracted, messy minds. We've gotten into the habit of paying attention to all the things our brain picks up, and there's a lot: Your subconscious brain is checking about five times every second to see if there is something relevant to heed. But we've taken what was once an evolutionary advantage and allowed it to distract us repeatedly throughout the day, even when we're in very safe environments, since the amygdalae are scanning for both positive and negative things of importance.

I see this attentional pull in airports as I watch people check their smartphones for texts or emails. I'm guilty of it too. It is astonishing how often we go back to check to see if someone has contacted us. Technology unleashes us to be free to do many things and, paradoxically, it's also one of the greatest harnesses of our time. It keeps us from noticing things—the things we see when we focus, like how the raisin tastes and feels, the noises in the room we never noticed, our body discomforts, and a variety of other things.

The great news is that many pieces of research[11, 12, 13] show that the specific activity of being in our ECN is associated with keeping the normal atrophy of our brain's gray matter at bay, and in some cases, even thickening it. Gray matter is the matter of the brain that is involved in processing and cognition. It atrophies as we age; but in many cases, it doesn't have to as rapidly as it often does. In one study, researchers found that subjects who engaged in mindfulness activities, such as the raisin exercise, for about twenty-five minutes each day for eight weeks experienced an increase in the thickness of their gray matter.[14] That means that taking a few minutes each day, even if they have to be broken into smaller five- or ten-minute chunks, can help us keep up our brain capacity well into old age. It also benefits the brain and gives us a sense of well-being by bringing down our cortisol, calming the threat response, slowing our breathing, and leveling out our blood pressure. It's like a mental eraser of all the crud going on around us.

The raisin activity trains us to stay in the present. I suggest getting a box of raisins and putting them next to your desk as a reminder to take some downtime. Even if the raisin doesn't work for you, requiring yourself to stay focused on one thing a few times a day, no matter how you do it, can benefit *all* of your work. It's a form of willpower, and we need practice to stay focused. Start with the raisin ninety seconds twice a day. Increase it as you can. See how much ECN time you can get in. I'd love to hear about your results. If you feel hesitant to do it, remember our mantra: start small, start now.

It is worth mentioning that there is a downside to intense focus. Too much focus can cause us to miss social cues around us. I remember doing a feedback session with a businessman whose employees' chief complaint was that he would walk down the hall and never address them. He'd never say, "How's it going, Denise?"—he wouldn't even give a hello. They labeled him as a callous, uncaring leader and said that the morale in the department reflected that popular notion of this leader. When I told him this, he was so visibly shaken that you would have thought I had burped in his face. I had him reflect on his jaunts through the office and asked what he did as he walked the halls. Then it hit him. He said he was usually so absorbed in reading his myriad printed emails as he made his way from meeting to meeting that he didn't even notice his surroundings. He said he cared *very* much about his employees and that this news mortified him. This is a perfect case of focus being a detriment. Overfocus happens in sports as well, when players lose track of time and thus miss critical moments to score against opponents during a close game.

As with nearly all the concepts in the book, focus isn't an all-or-nothing proposition. Sometimes, it makes sense to focus intently, and other times, it makes sense to switch between that intensity and a broader attention of the world. Focus when you are working on something specific, especially something that requires accuracy. Also focus when listening to someone. Most times when you're in public, allow your attention to broaden so you can see the bigger picture and pick up on important cues from the environment.

ACTIVATION

- Get a stopwatch. Try the raisin exercise. Start the watch when you begin the exercise and only look at it again the first time your mind wanders off the raisin. You might only be able to go ten seconds, but you'll get better with practice. Each day, practice going longer and longer until you can get to several minutes without wandering.

- While exercising on the elliptical, wear headphones and listen to music that inspires you. Avoid watching a TV while doing this. When you feel safe and comfortable on the elliptical machine, try to close your eyes for an entire song. It's more difficult than it sounds.

• Create a work environment that allows you to focus. Maybe low light makes you feel unfrenzied, so get a lamp in your office. Close your door. Turn off anything that can contact you while you're focusing. If light background music is permissible in your work area and it helps you focus, add that to the mix.

AN ABUNDANCE MENTALITY IMPROVES OUR WILLPOWER

Having an abundance mentality could change the course of your life. I used to hear about it mostly in the speeches of motivational speakers or read about it in self-help books. The idea of it lies in the belief that "there is more where that came from" as opposed to the scarcity mentality: You have to get everything you can right now so someone else doesn't take it first.

While scarcity thinking zaps us of many positive attributes, abundance mentality does the opposite. Abundance is about thinking on the positive side of the chart, and in case you've missed the message, the positive side of life is generally better for your brain and your relationships, for your business and for the rest of your life. Because the brain's ability to detect threat and danger far outperforms the reward capacities of the brain, it is important to keep a deliberate eye on the positive possibilities; otherwise, you can become overwhelmed with hypervigilance, obsessing about what's wrong and what you don't have—a sure knock to your confidence.

The abundance mentality is surely an inspirational and pleasant way to think about life in general. But now, emerging neuroscience shows us that beliefs about abundance may create tangible, positive outcomes. A scarcity mentality, on the other hand, has been shown to have the opposite effect. Even more startling is the fact that it actually can affect our IQ. Harvard and Princeton University researchers Sendhil Mullainathan and Eldar Shafir show in their book *Scarcity: Why Having Too Little Means So Much* that overloading the executive center of the brain with worries about what we don't have has a negative effect on our general intelligence. The implications of this can affect our short-term cognitive capacity, overall life success, decision making, and energy levels. It can also have an effect on one of the most powerful tools we can wield—willpower.

Researchers have found that we can extend our mental energy if we change our beliefs about our ability to keep on going, even when we feel like we want to give up. It was proven in a small but elegant study, again at Stanford University, that our beliefs about willpower can lead us to keep on going.[15] The researchers primed one set of subjects with the belief that willpower is abundant and the other with the belief that willpower is exhaustible, and they found that this priming of the beliefs predicted how well the subjects did on difficult memory tasks, with the abundance group performing better.

There are many uses for this theory in our work and personal lives. Think about how exhausting it is to work on a deadline that goes late into the evening (hopefully that's not standard for you). Next time it happens, try retraining yourself to think that this kind of hard work is energizing and that your brain is growing; it could affect your stamina. I call it the "bring it on" mentality. It's a notion leaders could instill in their teams: that when things get tough, that's when we're really good. It might sound trite, but framing difficulty in a positive light can pump us up and energize us. You just have to choose abundance over scarcity.

ACTIVATION

- The next time you feel like your energy is being zapped by a long to-do list, stop and take a break. Then make sure you have nourished and hydrated yourself properly. Next, reframe all of the work staring at you. Tell yourself, "This is when I'm at my best! If this was easy, anyone could do my job."

- Listen to your self-talk when you're overwhelmed. Are you sabotaging yourself by saying things like "This work is ridiculous" or "This is getting out of hand"? Try saying something like this instead: "Okay, this is hard, but I'm fully equipped to manage this."

Willpower is also, of course, an essential ingredient in achieving the goals we need and want to achieve. Read on to find out more.

CHAPTER 7

Goal Achievement

THINK ABOUT YOUR TO-DO LIST. When you get something done on it, do you just move on to the next item, or do you cross out the completed item? The very act of checking something off the list gives us a dopamine bump, and then we want to do it again. It's one of the reasons why Weight Watchers and similar programs work so well. I've said it before and I'll say it again: The brain is a completion machine. It loves getting things done and rewards us with a good feeling—that dopamine bump—when we do.

Steven Stein, one of the foremost voices in the field of emotional intelligence, was once asked what he thought defined success. He said that success is—in its narrowest definition—when someone sets daily goals and achieves them. Stein says that in essence, if someone who was begging for money on the street corner set a goal to earn $15 before noon and was successful in accomplishing that, he or she would be considered successful. Typically, success is thought of as achieving bigger, more elaborate goals, but Stein challenges us to look at success differently.

The power of having goals lies in the simple idea that we get what we want in life when we set and achieve objectives for ourselves, and in the grander notion that achieving goals sets off a cascade of neurochemistry that leads us toward well-being. Those who set goals report higher happiness and overall well-being than those who set no goals at all.[1,2] And achieving small goals has about the same neuro-reward as achieving big ones (cleaning out a closet that's been staring at you for months can feel just about as good, brain-wise, as getting a promotion that you've worked for). The neurochemical reward of achieving a goal doesn't last very long, though, so we want to replenish our goals if we want to continue to feel the dopamine bump that achieving them gives. Thus, life-long accomplishment of goals could be a factor in brain health, and it certainly is for our well-being.

Yet all too often—possibly daily—we operate with tiny little paper cuts of anxiety that keep throbbing, alerting us that we're not "getting things done." It can paralyze us and prevent us from starting on any substantial tasks on our list. Sometimes, we miss achieving a goal because too many obstacles and distractions get in the way. We can't complete the behaviors necessary to achieve the goal because we are completing other behaviors necessary to deal with the distractions. If we live too many days without completing our goals because there are so many competing priorities, it seems like we'll never achieve our bigger goals, and that is very likely true. Eventually, your life can feel like it is spinning out of control.

In this chapter, I'll share what we've learned about goal achievement, offer a way to refine and prioritize your goals, and give you some systems for achieving your goals and for setting parameters in your life that will help you achieve more of what you want.

WHY AND HOW: THE MECHANISMS OF GOAL ACHIEVEMENT

When your progress toward a goal gets really challenging, have you ever asked yourself, "Why am I doing this?" According to neuroscience, it's a very good thing if we ask the question. It is one of the two critical questions that can help us attain our goals: "Why?" and "How?" Neuroscientists at UCLA experimented with subjects and had them do a simple task, like brushing their teeth.[3] The group was asked to think about how, and then in a separate moment, think about why to brush their teeth as they did it. The results showed that the why and how activate two very different neural circuits. Interestingly, the results of the study also suggest that when one of the operations was on, the other was not. They found that the how and why are both parts of achieving the goal. We naturally switch back and forth between the how circuitry and the why circuitry as we work toward a goal—even one as basic as successfully brushing our teeth.

This has significant ramifications and tells us about the ingredients necessary for achieving our own goals, as well as how we can help our colleagues and others achieve theirs. University of Oregon psychology professor Elliot Berkman has written extensively on the hierarchy of motivation.[4,5] He points out that in order to remain motivated, we need both the how and the why. The why is the higher-order thinking that sits at the top of the motivational hierarchy, while the how is on the bottom, and more tactical.

Everything we do with intention is goal achievement. As far as the brain is concerned, successfully making it to the restroom is a goal achieved. For more intentional goals, like hitting sales targets or completing a project ahead of deadline, the path to successful completion isn't always as clear or easy as the simpler goals, like getting a cup of coffee.

Berkman says that when we get stuck in the details of a project and feel anxious or exhausted from all there is to do, we can possibly boost our motivation by taking a moment to move up into the "why" region of the brain, reminding ourselves why we are toiling so hard. For example, you might say to yourself during a difficult period at work that you're doing all of this so your kids can go to a good college and so you can have a nice retirement. On the other hand, when we have the why of a goal firmly set but find ourselves spinning our wheels and getting no closer to achieving it, we can benefit from moving down the motivational hierarchy to the how—the small activating activities that get us going. As simple as this research makes goal achievement sound, sometimes we get in our own way and we need a system.

USE A SYSTEM TO BREAK LONG-TERM GOALS INTO SHORT-TERM ACCOMPLISHMENTS

Okay, so I've done it. I've created a cheesy acronym. I started it when writing about goal achievement in my previous book, *Be a Shortcut*, in which I described the STTARR model:

- **See** the goal; visualize it. Also, write it down. People who write their goals down are more likely to accomplish them.
- **Touch** on something to do with the goal every day.
- **Think** about how the last step toward the goal went.
- **Adjust** what you're doing if necessary.
- **Reward** yourself in small ways to keep yourself going.
- **Repeat** until you've achieved your goal.

I've now made a neuroscience-informed modification of the model. The main elements are still there, but the model now includes *activation*—in other words, starting small, starting now—as the first component, so it's ASTTARR. You, too, can be ASTTARR! Remember, you might not want to clean out the garage, but you want it clean. That's where activation, your kick-start—comes in. Starting small and starting now is critical to get things going in this model.

Using a system like this one can help us because it keeps us focused on the step immediately in front of us. Research has shown that goals that are too distant in the future are less likely to be accomplished unless we break them down into more bite-sized pieces that we can work on now.[6] An interesting phenomenon that occurs in our brain might explain why we're less likely to accomplish goals set too distant in the future—ninety days or more. Try this: Think about all the things you need to accomplish in the next week or so. You can even write them down if you haven't already put them on a list. When you think of those to-do items—those goals—an area in your brain activates that also switches on when you think about yourself and when you think about people who are like you. We often have a better relationship with people who are like us because we can better mentalize, or think about what they might be thinking. When we think about the not-too-distant goals on our list, it seems that we have a better relationship with the goals because we can mentalize and see ourselves accomplishing them. However, when a goal is set further out than about ninety days, a different part of our brain activates—the same one that activates when we think about someone who is unlike us.[7] That dissimilarity can make it more difficult to mentalize and reach agreement. It can feel bad, making us want to get away. Those goals that are too far in the future apparently look like a dissimilar person to the brain, so it's possible that we don't see ourselves accomplishing them. That's why we may sabotage ourselves and put off doing anything to achieve the goal, or at the very least wait until the last minute, when we're under pressure to perform.[8]

Thus, neuroscience suggests that we take those big, long-term goals and break them down into smaller, closer goals. Think about it like this. If you decide that you want to be fifty pounds lighter five months from now, your brain's likely to say, "You're joking" and act as if you're unlikely to accomplish that goal. Better to reduce the goal into a set of manageable goals that we can check off as we progress; each small step will give us a dopamine bump and encourage us forward. These tiny steps prove to the brain that the goal is indeed our own, and then we are more likely to proceed with our goal; without the small steps, we are likely to remain the same. So you see that reaching your goals is all about starting small and starting now. Use a system like ASTTARR to make the transition from going for a grand jackpot to picking up daily prizes as you go.

REFINE YOUR LIST TO IMPROVE YOUR ODDS

One of the biggest wastes of energy and resources is keeping little things we need to remember floating around in our prefrontal cortex (PFC). Remember, the PFC is a big, complex, and powerful tool, and asking it to hang on to phone numbers and errands and other trivial scraps of information is akin to using a fishing net in the ocean when all we're looking for is one goldfish. It's not a very wise use of our resources. The PFC will remember much of the information for the short term, but it is overkill. You bog it down and prevent it from handling bigger, more important things. It will have a lot to do, but it won't do any of it particularly well. Eventually, the PFC becomes overtaxed and starts dropping bits of data. The PFC is not an inexhaustible resource for these small fragments of information. That's when we forget that we were supposed to pick up an anniversary card on the way home from work.

We don't have to make big choices to make big things happen in our life. If we have a project looming, the very act of deliberately choosing not to do it right now, to tell it to stand down and not rear its ugly head while we attend to what we deem a more important issue, is a choice, and one that will go a long way toward managing our anxiety around the task. The physical energy it takes for the brain to manage multiple competing tasks is considerable, and making a firm decision on which item to begin gets us activated and going.

Try this. Write down everything that you can think of that you need to do that is looming before you. Nothing is too trivial—things like calling your mom, cleaning the garage, getting the oil changed in the car, getting a haircut, sending a birthday card, buying an anniversary gift, getting the expense report done, and so on. Now check off the ones you probably would never have written down because you just assumed they were important enough to remember—they're the "of course" items that you rely on your PFC to keep track of. There's a lot of them, right? All these trivial items bombard our PFC on a daily basis. The magnitude of things our brain sorts and sifts is astonishing.

Researcher Malia Mason[9] has found that the way we approach big goals is similar to the way the brain carries out smaller motor goals, like doing the laundry. When you tell yourself that you need to do laundry, you don't have to actively think about how to do it; a chain of events begins and the brain starts working to complete the goal. Of course, there are hundreds of steps that happen in the brain to achieve even the simplest goal, but the brain keeps the series going until the task is complete. Mason wondered if larger objectives work the same way. Indeed, she found that when we give ourselves a more complex goal, like writing a report, we initiate a chain of events in our brain that don't fully end until we complete the goal. When we stop moving toward the goal, the brain is still waiting in the background to continue. Because it still wants to complete the sequence, the brain may pull our attention away from what we're working on and say, "Hey! You! Over here! You still have that birthday gift to buy; do you want to buy this little trinket you just saw on the billboard you just passed?" Have you ever been talking to someone when all of a sudden you are reminded of something so random and so urgent that you can't ignore it? That's what a messy brain looks like—distracted and unable to accomplish the task in front of it because it's got a host of priorities floating around. The messy brain is being pulled toward competing open orders in a sort of masochistic tug-of-war.

This multiple-goal challenge also applies to corporations. Many companies have "ten critical initiatives" or "fourteen pillars of achievement" that need to be completed in the next four quarters, and they often push and pull employees in the same confusing way. When asked to recite their corporate priorities, the vast majority of employees are at a loss (and remember, one of the defining characteristics of activation is that clarity about the steps to be taken can lead to motivation). Given that compensation may also be attached to these large and nebulous lists, it's no wonder so many people are overwrought, distracted, and missing targets at work. Leaders can do themselves, their employees, and their shareholders an enormous favor by focusing on a few achievable things at a time. As one very enlightened leader recently said, "We used to ask you to do more with less. Now we are asking you to do less, better."

How can individuals reduce the mental tug-of-war that happens when we have a ton of little things to remember? Changing your relationship with the items on your to-do list is a great place to start. Start deliberately telling your brain how much attention you want it to pay to each item rather than telling it to attend to many different things with no special emphasis. If you take the latter approach, your brain will try to attend to everything and do none of it particularly well.

David Allen's classic *Getting Things Done* contains great advice on organizing tasks that ties into this concept. But if you just need a quick starter, here's a popular and easy-to-remember tool called the 5 Ds. It's been hanging around in management circles for decades and there are many versions of it, but here's my take.

The 5 Ds

Put each of the things you need or want to do into one of the following five buckets:

- DO—this is reserved for things you can check off the list today.
- DELEGATE—this is for things you need done now or soon but that you can either delegate to a colleague or hire someone else to do. You don't do it, but you need it done. If you delegate to a subordinate,

be careful that you are keeping an eye on their open-order list as well as yours.

- DELAY—this is the unfortunate dumping ground for many items on the list that you need done but don't want to do yourself and don't have anyone you can delegate to. My rule is if the item stays on your list longer than ninety-six hours—four days—you'll most likely procrastinate and end up having a burst of anxiety every time you're reminded that you don't have it done. This is a time waster and a thorn in your side. If your list is full of these items, you're probably very anxious or at the very least discontented. Look at that item and have a discussion with yourself. Do you really want it done? Does it *have* to be done because of a work expectation? If the answer is yes to either, it's time to break down the item into something you'll do today so that you can begin to get the momentum you need. Create an activation. Start small, but start now. No, really, *now*! Or . . .

- DISCARD IT. If you can't do it or delegate it, and you keep delaying it and won't or can't create minigoals to achieve it—toss it away! Imagine the relief you'll feel. Imagine that your brain is saying, "Thank you for allowing me to *not* focus on that irritating little item anymore. Thank you, thank you. Now on to bigger assignments you actually want or need to accomplish."

- DREAM. The fifth D is my favorite and it might become yours, too. Write down one thing you want to accomplish before you leave this planet. Dream big, but make it something you actually want and can achieve. Don't say you want to take a trip to Mars. Things that have come up in my workshops include learning to play piano, guitar, or flute; learning to flamenco dance; learning a new language; visiting every continent; getting a face lift; owning a fly-fishing store on a small island—cool, inspirational goals like that. It doesn't matter what it is. It just matters that you *write it down*. I would put it on the bottom of my to-do list every single day. Transfer it every day to your list. The dream item is a goal that could be years off, but it is okay because you have told your brain, "I see myself accomplishing this, just not today."

That final D—the Dream category—merits a little further discussion. Since your brain attends to what you tell it to attend to, if your dream is on your list, your dream gets a little attention as an open order. It's not the annoying one tapping you on the shoulder, nagging you to get it done. It's an open order that you've directed your brain to be alert to, but as a long-term priority. Every time you see the goal on your list, you may be reinforcing your belief that the goal is achievable in your life. Additionally, you've primed your brain to see it in the environment. If learning to play the guitar is on your dream list, then it is likely that most every time you hear a guitar riff or you see someone play the guitar or talk about playing it, your brain will attend to that. You're more likely to ask questions, and your curiosity could very well act like a dog's nose, taking you to places you never thought possible.

As an added bonus, the Dream category could have a halo effect on the rest of your life. Viktor Frankl was a Nobel Prize–winning author and a survivor of Auschwitz.[10] After his liberation from the camp, he became a psychologist. He was most interested in the difference between survivors of the camps who came out intact and ready to conquer the world and get on with their lives and those who survived but with broken spirits. After much research and many interviews, he found the difference: Those who were still alive mentally had envisioned something they hoped for when they got out of the camp. They imagined themselves opening a new shop or getting married or moving to a new land. They had meaning. They had a "why." They had a dream. Frankl went on to develop logotherapy, which literally means "meaning therapy," to help depressed patients search for something to look forward to in their lives.

My philosophy is that I always like to have the ticket for my next vacation in my top desk drawer so that when I open it up, I get a little dopamine bump that positively affects my entire life. The Dream category can do that for you as well, and the more you bring your dream toward reality—getting brochures, cutting out pictures, or establishing a savings account—the more that little bump can affect all of your life. Dream big. Start doing something toward your dream. Start small, but start now.

GET HELP TO ACHIEVE

Robert Cialdini, an expert in influence psychology, has written about something called the commitment and consistency theory.[11] The gist of it is that we behave more consistently with goals that are

- Public. Tell others about the goal you set.
- Active. Do something about it. Write it down. Detail the steps.
- Effortful. We critically think about how it will affect our lives or we might get someone to hold us accountable to working on the goal.

The public and effortful aspects of Cialdini's model are confirmed by the Hawthorne effect,[12] which refers to the fact that we perform better when we know someone else is watching. Enlist trusted friends and colleagues in your life who will "watch" you. These are different than the people who have to watch you, like your boss (although your boss can serve as a cheerleader, too). The research shows that when we are public, active, and effortful about our intentions, they become reality more often—otherwise they're likely to stay as nagging little open orders.

Bluma Zeigarnik was a psychopathologist who, in the early twentieth century, witnessed a brain phenomenon similar to the Hawthorne effect. She discovered that we hold information in mind more readily when it is surrounded with "psychic tension"[13]—in other words, when we know we're going to be tested or that someone is watching. The watcher doesn't have to be another human: Take language-learning system Rosetta Stone, which tracks the user's progress through each module and has them go back and relearn a lesson if the student hasn't mastered it.

Accountability isn't just a corporate buzzword: It works because our brain knows we are being watched. See what happens when you get an accountability buddy of your own.

WHEN YOUR SANITY IS THE GOAL: SETTING PARAMETERS WE CAN LIVE BY

Phyllis was a high-level, very analytical, and self-reportedly cynical executive who was wracked with cancer. When I met her, she was in the final six months of her life. During one of our discussions, Phyllis said something very wise that seems to apply to individuals and their companies. She said, "I thought growth was about having the great house, furniture, and fine cars. I thought it was about becoming highly degreed and exquisitely pedigreed and having a great income. But in the end, I see that growth is not so much about adding on as it is about letting go. That's when you really soar, when you let go of obstacles in your life so that you can meet your true self again."

That's Phyllis's candid, crystal-clear appraisal of setting parameters and reacquainting ourselves with what is really important to all aspects of our lives. Her lesson is that sometimes our best choice might be decluttering our world, letting go of so many of the things we said yes to because they made sense way back then but that don't make sense now. She was talking about establishing parameters that allow us to flourish instead of being in that tug-of-war mentioned earlier that can lead to a less fulfilling, less productive life.

Take stock of whether you feel like you have clear parameters as you go about your day. Does your office feel like it has a revolving door attached, and in each of the door's compartments are people who want different things from you? Does your calendar feel like a free-for-all? Do you ever get schedule creep, where you know you said yes to some committee or event, but when the day of reckoning comes you can't figure out why you said yes with all that you've got going on? If so, the parameters of your life have been breached—and the only person who can put the walls back up is you.

Setting healthy parameters is a path to goal achievement and overall well-being. The parameters are something that can drive what goes on in your 5 Ds. When we understand where our lines are, we become better at controlling our days. What things are you saying no to by saying yes to other things? Of course there are the obligatory yeses because of choices we made a long time ago, like all of the things that go with kids and relationships and careers. But the happiest people with the healthiest brains are leaving space in their lives to say yes to themselves as well. It isn't too much to say yes to ourselves every day. In order to do this, we just have to set parameters.

I often ask participants in my workshops, "How many of you do email or some form of work past eight o'clock in the evening on a regular basis?" At least half the class raises their hand every time. It is startling, because these are often the same people who grumble about having no time to spend with their partners and children, no time to do the hobbies they like. And yet, they *choose* to say yes to work and no to themselves, their family, their friends, and fun activities. They save it all up for the weekend, which of course only really consists of about thirty-six hours, because the march back to work begins for most of us on Sunday afternoon or evening. I've heard many reasons for this round-the-clock work schedule: "I have a big job with people all over the world and I need to be available almost twenty-four hours a day," "I have way more on my plate than I can ever get done in a day and it has to be done and I have to be the one to do it," and "I get paid a lot and I have a lot of responsibility," and, and, and . . . Of course those are all valid reasons, but really? Always saying yes to work and no to yourself? The messy parameters aren't just about work creeping into your personal life. It goes both ways. Setting parameters will likely positively affect all aspects of your life.

Of course, there are seasons in life where one domain requires more attention than others. That's the rhythm of life. Sometimes family is going to get a ton of attention because we just had a baby or our elderly parents need us or a loved one has a devastating disease. Sometimes we take that work assignment knowing full well that for two years we will be neck-deep in work and won't be able to hang out with friends at the pub or do full weekends with cookouts and movies and concerts. However, when the dust has settled, where do our priorities actually stand? When we get used to the incredible pace and we just live with it, our parameters become fuzzy. When we reacquaint ourselves with our boundaries, we can begin to set healthy parameters. If we don't, it becomes all too easy to become addicted to the craziness and start thinking that that's the way life is.

On the A&E TV show *Hoarders*, specialists help people afflicted with hoarding disorder using a combination of compassion and tough love. It's really difficult to get some of those deeply afflicted with hoarding to let go of their things—even if it's trash. In one episode, a psychologist was on-site helping a guy (we'll call him Bill) sort through things and toss them away. It wasn't a good scene. Bill had an excuse for keeping everything, including screws and trash and random receipts for socks he bought eight years ago. Finally, the psychologist had a laser-like tough love discussion with Bill. He asked Bill how much he loved his family. Bill responded with "They mean everything in the world to me." Now the psychologist had a relative weight on his family's importance and was able to use it to make Bill determine whether to keep or toss things. Bill's family had brought about this intervention and were ready to cut Bill out of their lives if it didn't work; they believed that his affliction would eventually affect Bill's grandchildren. As Bill picked up each item and began to come up with some reason for why he should keep it, the psychologist would ask him, "On a scale of one to ten, with seven being the importance of keeping your family, where do you rate this item?" Well, that was a real predicament for Bill. As they slogged through his heaps of junk, Bill was asked to rate a hedge trimmer without a cord. "Eight!" he said. "I can fix that!"

"So you'd place the hedge trimmer above your family?" the psychologist asked.

As you might imagine, Bill reevaluated and ended up rating away nearly all of his piles. He was talked into only keeping those things that rated a five and above.

I'm hoping you're not as attached to the clutter—literal and figurative—in your life, but this rating method is a simple and interesting way to set your parameters.

ACTIVATION

Following are some of the things to rate on a scale of one to ten, with eight being the number you assign to the item of the most value to you at this point in time (this gives you room to grow and change if need be!).

Next to each item below, write your rating and think about how that rating affects the amount of time you're willing to spend on that item.

▢	Life partner	▢	Career
▢	Children	▢	Mom/Dad
▢	Brothers/Sisters	▢	Friends
▢	Email	▢	Your home
▢	God	▢	Religion
▢	Leisure travel	▢	Pets
▢	Your car	▢	Your looks
▢	Your health	▢	Food
▢	Money	▢	Politics
▢	Status	▢	Anything else you want to add

Now look back on your ratings. Are you spending the largest amounts of time on the most highly rated items? Most of us will see some misalignment here. Don't beat yourself up over this. You might be in a season of your life where something that wouldn't normally be your highest priority is now on top of the list. But be equally as honest about whether you are allowing your fives to become your eights on a regular basis, thus choosing a life that's most out of balance for you.

Once you've gotten an honestly rated list going, it's time to put those ratings into action as a living, breathing treatise of your life—your parameters in action. With your rated list in hand, pinpoint which items hold a mismatch between the time you spend and the rating you gave. If your partner is most important to you and you see that you've placed work above him or her, this is where an activation for change is probably required. Or maybe you say that working out is high on your list, but you're so exhausted from working so much that you don't do it. You say your kids are important, but you're so busy on emails at home that you talk to the kids while looking at a computer screen. You say that getting a promotion is a priority and yet you don't take any time to increase your skill and knowledge. There are so many ways to be off our game that deliberately choosing becomes critical for a healthy existence.

Here's an example of choosing parameters.

My friend Jason sits on a volunteer board of directors. He bounced the following scenario off me and asked if he was setting appropriate parameters. The board president (let's call him Charlie) is a go-getter and committed to the organization—his life is at a six, his career at a seven, and the organization is sometimes at an eight, according to Jason's estimation. He appointed Jason to lead a major committee because Jason showed some interest in the topic, but beyond that Charlie and Jason didn't have a discussion about it. Within a few days of getting back from the board meeting, Jason began to get pounded by emails from Charlie asking what he was going to do and saying that he needed to call Charlie tomorrow between ten in the morning and two in the afternoon. Jason emailed him to tell him that he was in client meetings that day and was not available until next Wednesday, five days hence. Charlie emailed back and said that he was available over the weekend and in the late evenings—in fact, Jason should call him tonight as late as one in the morning. Charlie said that, given his own availability, there was no excuse for Jason not to call him. That's when Jason's parameter-setting kicked in.

Jason told Charlie that he doesn't do volunteer board business past six in the evening or on weekends unless it's an emergency, and seeing that the volunteer organization doesn't save people's lives, Jason couldn't imagine it was an emergency. Jason told him next Wednesday at ten in the morning would be the best he could do. Charlie scheduled the time and when they talked, he asked near the end of their discussion how Jason got away with "putting things off" for so long. Jason told Charlie he wasn't putting things off; he was just putting other things on, and that in terms of where this volunteer business fell in his life, eight being the most important, this was a three or four. Jason detailed for him the myriad things that ranked higher. Charlie was astonished, but not appalled. He asked how Jason was so clear on that, and Jason told him about how he sets parameters. When you have clear parameters, it clarifies most choices and makes them so much easier to make.

Creating parameters that we can live with and that are appropriate for our work is critical for control. Please get out your calendar and your to-do list. Remember that your brain works best when it isn't cluttered with various remnants of undone tasks and meetings we need to attend. Write things down and find a way to prioritize and organize in a way that consistently works for you.

ACTIVATION

- Say no to one thing that might intrude on your personal time this weekend. Reserve that gained time for something that's more important to you than the thing you said no to.

- Start your list of the 5 Ds.

- Look at your current goals and break them down into smaller, shorter-term goals.

- Create a wall calendar that you can use to check off completed subgoals on your way to the larger goal.

- Celebrate milestones.

- Inventory the big things you're involved with now—working on multiple committees at work, coaching the soccer team, taking piano lessons, taking on yet another charity board. Look at the items you've said yes to that might need to be retired. Toss them out or transition them out of your life.

- Do something today that gives you a sense of control, such as pampering yourself, cleaning a drawer, going on a walk for as long as *you* think you should, choosing to read something *you* want to read, or watching something on TV that *you* want to watch.

Sometimes to grow we have to let go. It's interesting how we can all benefit from someone tapping us on the shoulder and reminding us to get back to ourselves, to free the brain up from juggling so many things that aren't making us better. Once we get to a simpler place, we can—somewhat paradoxically— be more available for other possibilities, for things that invigorate, interest, inspire, and calm us.

There is only so much room in life for all of our things, and contrary to myth, our brain is not an unlimited collector of the multitudes of bits and pieces—at least the well-functioning brain isn't. Let go to grow.

Let's capitalize on the new sense of energy and control that setting parameters gives us and use that momentum to create stamina.

3

Building Your Stamina

CHAPTER 8

Stamina, Stress, and Your Brain

SEVERAL YEARS AGO, I bought a twenty-five-foot blue spruce tree for my yard. I was given instructions on how to care for the tree. I was given a one-year warranty on it, too. Couldn't you predict that one year and one week later, the spruce went brown and lost every one of its needles? Being a costly tree, I called the nursery and told them what I was looking at. They sent an arborist. He asked why I hadn't called sooner. I told him the needles literally just turned brown and dropped the past week. He continued to ply me with questions about my care of the tree. When I told him how I watered it, he told me that the tree, according to the instructions they had given me, needed more attention during its first year in the ground, to help it get established. He said it didn't die last week; it had died six months ago. He said they just look good until they don't anymore, and then they drop everything.

That reminds me of the human brain. We go and go and go and overflood our brain with activity and distractions and intensity without resting it or paying attention to its basic needs. And it looks good for the most part—until it doesn't anymore. Somewhere along the way, beginning centuries ago, we started to tell ourselves a tall tale about the stamina of our brain. We bought into the myth that our thinker would be available anytime we wanted it and that it was an inexhaustible resource. We've discovered that this is wrong. If we put ourselves under unrelenting stress, if we're not properly resting and refueling, we may shrink and age our brain without even knowing it until it's too late. And in the short term, we simply exhaust it, which affects us cognitively, emotionally, and physically. We limit our stamina, often when we seem to need it the most. That is the paradox.

Take a look at the definition of the word *stamina*:

> Stamina. noun. The ability to sustain prolonged physical or mental effort. Synonyms: endurance, staying power, tirelessness, fortitude, strength, energy, toughness, determination, tenacity, perseverance, grit **(Oxford English Dictionary— Oxforddictionaries.com)**

After reading that definition, can you say you don't want stamina—or any of its synonyms—for yourself? *Stamina* is the beautifully inclusive word that sums up how most of us would like to approach our work, and life in general. It's critical if we want to succeed. As a matter of fact, researchers have found that a word synonymous with stamina—grit—is what separates those who succeed in achieving difficult goals from those who don't. Grit is about perseverance and passion for long-term goals. Chief researcher Angela Duckworth writes, "the achievement of difficult goals entails not only talent but also the *sustained and focused application* of talent over time."[1] Duckworth and her colleagues found that grit—stamina—is at least as important to high achievement as talent. In other words, without stamina, goals might just be a nice idea. The energy to keep on going is essential in a work world filled with multiple long-term goals and competing priorities.

Science and medicine have enabled us to keep on going, or at least keep on breathing, for longer than ever before. But being truly alive is about much more than being able to fog a mirror—it has to do with the vitality of our brain. And yet we often feel exhausted at the end of workdays, drained of the stamina we need to participate in the five or so hours remaining in the day. If we want more stamina in our lives, we need to start with our brain—to give it a break and tend to its needs daily.

Up until only a few years ago, we thought that the brain could not regenerate itself, but as we discussed in an earlier section on trying new things, we now know that with proper care, the brain does continue growing and reshaping itself throughout life. Our ability to reshape the brain, known as *neuroplasticity*, and our ability to generate new neurons in certain areas of the brain, known as *neurogenesis*, grow when we focus, rest, and exercise (both physically and mentally) the brain. In fact, everything we do—learning, thinking, feeling, experiencing, talking, and behaving—causes structural changes on the neuronal level. Be careful about what you think, say, and do!

Yet most of us seem to struggle with those basics. Instead, we often use our weekends and vacations for catching up on downtime and developing healthier habits. I've been on several vacations where the first few days are so devoted to catching up on rest that I can't remember much about them. I obviously needed the intense downtime, but I would've liked to participate more vigorously in my vacation. I couldn't, though, because I was so utterly tired.

But what if it didn't have to be that way? What if you could be present and energized before, after, and during work? What if your downtime was really "up time," where you expended an energy level of your choosing on something you enjoy, rather than plopping down with a heavy sigh?

The chapters in part III of this book are about giving yourself a fighting chance of deliberately directing your energy and increasing your stamina—and thereby increasing your confidence and control. There is no perfect formula for doing that. Everyone is different, after all. We each sleep differently, metabolize food differently, live differently. Some of us are contending with physical ailments that eat our energy and reduce our stamina. We all have different stress-inducing items on our to-do lists. These chapters are *not* about universal, immediate fixes (though some of the suggestions can make us feel better rapidly), but rather about how we can operate in a way that helps us confront the difficulties thrown at us by work and life from a stronger position. If we pay attention to our stress levels, our sleep, what we eat and drink, the messages we expose ourselves to every day, and the quality of our overall environment, we build a better foundation and give ourselves the stamina to handle the really messy days that are bound to happen. (As a word of caution, if you put all the tools discussed in these chapters to use and still feel exhausted or anxious, please consult your physician.)

Let's start building that foundation by exploring the role of stress in our lives.

STRESS

I met a businessman not long ago who shared a horrific story during a workshop. It helped illustrate how stress can help us and then hurt us, especially if we don't pay attention to the signals our brain is sending.

You may recall hearing about the attack in the Westgate shopping mall in Nairobi, Kenya, where terrorists killed seventy-two people on September 21, 2013. This businessman was there when it happened. He described the intense focus that came over him as he and others hid behind boxes of lightbulbs in the back room of one of the stores being targeted. He was able to stay calm and help quiet other shoppers who were frantic with fear, even covering some of them with his body. He was having a threat response, and that was the positive aspect of it. He explained how the cortisol and adrenaline came to his rescue and how he was able to operate deliberately and calmly, with a clear vision of what needed to happen in the mall that day.

Fast-forward four weeks, and he was in the leadership program telling his story and describing the overwhelming exhaustion he had been combating every day since the incident. Another effect of the threat response, but this time not so good. Unfortunately, his system had not calmed back down to normal, and he acknowledged that he was still replaying the events in his mind. This replay may have retriggered some of the stress response that, while useful to him in the moment, was definitely detrimental after the fact. Imagine your brain being on alert all of the time because you're replaying a negatively intense event you experienced. Imagine how tired you would become from this hypervigilance.

Hopefully, this businessman took our suggestion that he seek professional help to talk through the traumatic events in an attempt to recalibrate his "fight, flight, or freeze" system. The class listened with deep interest because, as some of them confided, they often felt the same way, even though they hadn't been exposed to such a horror. They were reliving stressful experiences, and the constant replaying was depleting their energy reserves.

Here's the important point: The brain doesn't necessarily sort out the content of the stresses in our life right away. As discussed in chapter 2, if we think we're being terrorized, our brain will oblige by switching on the neurochemistry that helps us survive. This is an appropriate reaction in a terrorist attack, but not to a negative situation in our everyday work and life. We are not designed to have our threat response on *all* of the time.

Stress can have both positive and negative effects on our success. Unfortunately, we have become so used to the idea of stress that many of us think very little about our relationship with it and whether we invite it into our lives. When we're under constant stress, our stamina suffers. We become tired and lethargic. The more we fail to manage the stress, the more stress comes to us uninvited. Recall that cortisol and other stress hormones exhaust our physical system over time—they are antistamina.

The first step is to check your own stress levels, covered in the next section of this chapter. When I feel exhausted and I can't point to an illness, I check the amount of negative stress I am perceiving. From there, we'll see how to pursue positive stress and mitigate the negative stress, and examine why our mindsets matter as we carry that out.

A STRESS CHECK

Let's get a reading on your stress level. Write down all of the things that stress you in your life this very moment. Nothing is too small or too large. Think about anything that gives you a little ping in your belly or causes you to give even the littlest of sighs. Don't be shy about including work deadlines, emails you haven't replied to, the performance review that's around the corner, the oil change light in your car, or an upcoming medical visit. As you look at your list, consider the items that may be boosting your cortisol. Also be aware of the items on your list that, while stressful, seem to be overall positive—they make you alert but in an energized way.

When reviewing your list, it's helpful to think in terms of what deserves the kind of intense neurochemical bath that negative stress brings on. Remember that the brain and body want to get back to balance as soon as possible; they want homeostasis. When do you relieve yourself of this barrage of stressors that play havoc with your brain? It can seem like we'll never get back to normal without taking a vacation. And yet, with vacation coming only a few times a year, these resets of the stress response aren't consistent enough to really help us stay mentally healthy or as productive as we could be. As with your to-do list, your stressor list deserves your awareness so you can put those gnawing worries into perspective and change your response to them. Some of the items on your to-do list may be the very things that cause you to feel some anxiety, so you might be killing two monsters with one stone; by managing your to-do list you may be alleviating some of the anxiety about things you would put on your stressor list.

Go back through your list and circle the things on it that *really, really* do require you to be on high alert. Do you have a presentation tomorrow that could win you a multimillion-dollar contract and a big fat bonus? That requires high alert. Do you have fifty unanswered emails—just like you've always had? That probably doesn't require high alert. You'll undoubtedly find that the list goes from tens of items to just a very few. Once you have your list whittled down, you can minimize your overall stress and even leverage your remaining items for brief spurts of positive stress throughout the day.

Years ago I worked as a television news producer, and I had a fellow producer who would have her news show pretty much finished and written hours before air. When other producers would ask her why she came in so early and worked to get the show nearly finished five hours before airtime, especially because changes would happen throughout the day, she would tell them that it was much easier to deal with the stress of some big story coming in ten minutes before airtime if everything else had been managed. It was so much easier to break apart the show if the foundation was solid. When it was messy and stories were unwritten, she said she couldn't get a good handle on which pieces to move, which to hold for another day's telecast, and which to discard altogether. Being prepared gave her a sense of control, and as you might remember, that's usually a better place from which to operate. She was controlling what she could control in order to better manage the stressors she knew would arrive.

If we don't pay heed to the stressors in our lives and do what we can to mitigate them, they can negatively affect our sleep, our ability to get waking rest, and our ability to be active. Unfortunately, those are also the very things that help us combat stress. It's a catch-22, and we have to get in front of it if we want our brain to be at its healthiest and our lives to be productive and happy. We'll talk more in coming chapters about how to get the best exercise, sleep, and waking rest so that stress doesn't drive negativity in your daily life.

THE RIGHT MINDSET CAN MAKE STRESS ENERGIZING AND PRODUCTIVE

As you seek to reduce stress and increase your stamina, here's a fascinating and helpful truth: The way you think about stress can positively predict your physiological response to it. Reframing how you think about stress can have a constructive impact on your brain and body. Much like how an abundance mindset can increase your willpower, stress chemicals are apparently affected by our beliefs about stress itself. In a study at Yale University, researchers tested about four hundred employees.[2] They assigned people randomly to a "stress is enhancing" group, a "stress is debilitating" group, or a control group that received no intervention. Their extraordinary findings show how we can increase our stamina in the face of stress:

- Researchers found that the prevalent belief among most people is that stress is debilitating.
- The brain is easily "primed" with messages—both positive and negative—about stress, and that priming affects how the brain functions. Researchers exposed participants to only ten minutes of video over a single week that put forth the assigned mindset (either enhancing or debilitating). That small amount was enough to change participants' mindsets.
- Those exposed to "stress is enhancing" messages reported greater well-being and work productivity.
- The "stress is debilitating" group reported no change in productivity or well-being, or in some cases *lower* well-being and/or productivity.

- The most stunning result was that the neurochemistry of participants mirrored the messages their groups were primed with: Enhancing beliefs reduced cortisol levels while debilitating beliefs increased cortisol levels.

The research illustrates that we can change our beliefs about stress, and that those beliefs affect our performance. This is a rallying cry for leaders to push a message that reinforces stress as a positive: "When things get difficult around here, that's when we're at our best."

As I was writing this book and feeling overwhelmed at how much rewriting was required from my first draft, my editor, Lari Bishop, wisely said, "Writing a book is supposed to be hard. This process is how good writers become great. It's hard and you get on with it anyway." That one line in her email to me literally reset my stress levels and boosted my confidence to keep on going.

So, on one hand we all know that stress *is* actually bad in some cases—when we're chronically stressed out, it can eat us alive. On the other hand, with the proper mindset, we can take spurts of intense stress and turn them into a stamina maker, something that actually rallies the best part of us to tackle the problem at hand.

As long ago as 1908, Robert Yerkes and John Dodson published a stress and performance theory that is still used today, appropriately named the Yerkes-Dodson law.[3] In essence, it says that when we are learning a task, as stress goes up, our performance does too—to a point. If we aren't aware of our breaking point, however, the stress hormone becomes overwhelming and the brain falls into a disorganized and anxious state. Our abilities suffer. We can see this when we're trying to teach a child a new skill. When they first try the new skill, it's all fun and games. But when pressed too long and hard to get better at it, the child devolves into crankiness and sometimes tears. They have a meltdown. We adults are not unlike that. We express the overstress differently, but we nevertheless excel to a point and then break apart in a similar fashion.

See if you can notice the fine line between these two sides of stress—when you're learning and energized and when you're overwhelmed and anxious. When you're in the negative state, the most useful thing to do is literally walk away and do something completely different for a while to help reset the stress response. Breathe, and try to be in the present, or leverage your ECN, which I described in the chapter on willpower. Being in the executive control state, fully absorbed in the present, has a tendency to calm our body's alarm system. Integrative neuroscientist Dr. Herbert Benson suggests that it only takes three deep abdominal breaths (the kind where your belly comes out when you breathe in) to calm us down from a state of nasty cortisol alarm and take us back to normal, where we can think and behave more thoughtfully.[4] Just before you perform a stress-inducing task—receiving a performance appraisal at work, presenting to the executive committee, taking a test, playing a tennis match or golf game, playing the piano at a recital—try taking three slow, deep breaths to calm yourself and put yourself in the moment. During any of those activities just mentioned, it's easy to fixate on how we might do in the future. Staying present, however, has been shown to produce better results and to lower our stress hormones.

Jim Komsa, vice president of sales at a Fortune 200 company, leads high-achieving teams in part because he intuitively understands the importance of mindset in the face of difficult challenges. When Jim inherited one new sales team, he told them about a horse trainer he'd worked with in an experiential leadership program. Jim explained that horses are extremely smart and very sensitive to the directions they receive, but the directives need to be unencumbered by fear and filled with confidence. Participants in this leadership program were asked to simply lift the horse's front hoof and clean its shoe. Jim described how surprisingly difficult it was; he couldn't get the horse to relinquish its hoof. The horse trainer took this failure as a teaching moment. He asked Jim to think about what he had been truly focused on during the exercise. Jim thought about it and acknowledged that he was thinking about all of his classmates sitting in the stands watching him, that he felt self-conscious and didn't want to lose. The horse trainer told him to reframe his thinking and focus his efforts completely on the horse, and that if he did so, he'd succeed at the task. The second time he tried, Jim was bewildered by how easily the horse lifted its hoof. Jim told this to his new sales team to impart a lesson: that reframing stressful events can lead to similar positive results. In this case, Jim reframed his efforts with the horse as a chance to immerse himself in learning a new task—rather than seeing it as the possibility of making a fool of himself in front of his peers.

ACTIVATION

- Go back to the stressor list I prompted you to create earlier in this chapter. Remember as you make your list to include even those items that stress you out only a little; even they can add to your cortisol load and lead to a major stressful blowout.

- Think about how much "stress juice" you are allowing each item on the list. If something doesn't deserve the intensity you've been giving it, notice the mismatch. Just the awareness that you're stressing about something more than it deserves can help reframe your view.

- Feeling stressed out is akin to feeling out of control. If you're feeling inordinately stressed out, consider rereading chapter 4.

- When you feel yourself getting stressed out and have determined that the stress is worth expending, tell yourself, "This is supposed to be hard. I actually get better working this hard."

- Note when you are learning from the edginess of stress. That means you're framing stress appropriately. Also note when you begin to break apart from too much stress. That's when it's time to take a break.

- Realize that you can have too much of anything, including positive stress.

It's not always easy to distinguish between positive and negative types of stress, but once you're aware of how much your mindset affects your performance in stressful situations, you're better equipped to make decisions about whether stress is an energy sucker or stamina maker.

Now, in the following chapters, we're going to look at ways to reduce and manage unnecessary negative stress—the kind that drains your brain, your productivity, and your sense of well-being—and build up your stamina.

CHAPTER 9

Quality In, Quality Out

IN ESSENCE, THE QUALITY of your day is reliant on your brain's energy level and the quality of its cells; when you have these, your stamina will increase, and you'll be able to manage stress better. But how do we ensure that we have plenty of energy and plenty of high-quality brain cells? These are determined in large part by what we put into our bodies. In fact, we can say that the health of your brain has a lot to do with what goes into the holes in your head: what you see, what you hear, what you breathe, what you smell, and what you eat and drink. All of these factor into brain health.

EATING AND DRINKING FOR THE BRAIN

Your body manufactures little of the fuel the brain uses to survive. The brain needs glucose and oxygen and a little fat and micronutrients. I like the metaphor of a car: Cars must have fuel, oil, oxygen, and water to operate. The brain, similarly, needs fuel in the form of glucose and some vitamins and minerals, oil in the form of oils and fats, plus oxygen and water. Since the body doesn't create these resources, and since there are even other bodily systems that compete for these resources, the brain can sometimes run low on them. When that happens, the brain prompts us to feed it by causing confusion, tiredness, irritability, and a number of other flags. Paying attention to how we feel and what our brain may need goes a long way toward our overall health—in particular, the stamina and acuity of the brain.

A couple of ground rules before we dive into looking at how to feed your brain:

- None of these recommendations are intended to replace any medical help you currently are or should be getting.
- These ideas are suggestions and are not intended to be exhaustive. There are thousands upon thousands of items that could be included on the lists of brain-healthy foods and drinks; included here are a few small things that could make a big difference. The suggestions are here to get you thinking about the fuel that goes in your body.
- "If two is good, four must be better" doesn't apply to the food and drink you ingest, even if you're eating something helpful. Please don't go out and eat two pounds of blueberries in one sitting. (Your stomach could have some not-so-good things to say about that.)
- Do what works for you. If you are allergic to something or your religion disallows something, there's no need to change. Take what works. Discard what doesn't. Make choices that work for you.

Water for Life

Hydration—simply drinking enough water—can be such a chore. I know it is for me. I often get to the end of the day and realize how little unadorned water I've consumed. I used to think it was enough that water is in coffee and beer and soda and anything wet we consume. So what if the water was coming in with other tasty things? But we've discovered that indeed it does matter: Those added extras sometimes act as diuretics, moving the fluid rapidly out of your system without a lot of uptake into the cells where it's needed. Plus, empty calories and side effects of sugar and alcohol come along with many drinks. Now I keep water bottles in my car and on my desk, and I always buy a bottle of water before boarding an airplane, because I know that flying is such a major dehydrator.

The average human needs six to eight eight-ounce glasses of water a day for the body to operate properly. The brain is approximately 75 percent water, so when we get dehydrated our brain function becomes worse, including memory.[1] Think about the parched people in the desert we see in the movies; they can't focus, they're hallucinating, their organs are basically shutting down to move available liquid to the heart and brain. That's an extreme example, and hopefully you don't become so dehydrated that you go into a fugue state at work, but lower-level dehydration can cause deleterious, and less noticeable, effects as well.

If your body is telling you you're thirsty, you're probably very dehydrated. When you feel parched, you know you've waited too long for a fill-up. Keep a water bottle at your desk and get into the habit of sipping from it throughout the day. (Cold water helps you burn more calories as your body heats up the liquid—good to know if you're trying to lose weight.) If you find yourself with a headache or leg cramps, try drinking water. Both of these accompany the lack of hydration.

Yes, drinking more water leads to more trips to the restroom. When this comes up, I always think of my dad when he was in his last days, having all manner of issues with body fluids moving properly in his system. It was everything we could do to get him to drink water. We tried to convince him that all of those trips to the restroom are the body's way of eliminating toxins. He didn't want to drink the water because it was too difficult to make it to the restroom that many times. The main theme of the end of his life was the fluid levels in his system. It's also the main theme of a healthy individual's life—it's just that we usually don't do something about it until we have a major health episode. The inconvenience of potty breaks is worth the payoff to your brain, not to mention your heart, liver, kidneys, hair, and skin. I've convinced myself to go grab a drink of water. Be right back.

Brain Food for Fuel

Okay, I've returned—now on to food. The brain needs carbohydrates in order to perform well; they are the source of glucose, the fuel for brain function. As with most things we consume, there's some controversy on this topic. Many fad diets prohibit carbohydrates in their initial stages and then add them back in the form of vegetables. While avoiding carbohydrates completely will certainly cause quick weight loss, it can be tough on the brain. Glucose that comes through complex carbohydrates keeps the brain operating. Complex carbs are those that occur in nature and can be found in almost any natural food we consume. What we want to avoid are simple carbs, found in things like candy, soda, breads, and most other manmade foods. They spike our blood sugar, and we're left dealing with the mental and physical crash that always follows. This wreaks havoc over time on the brain and body. Ask your physician or a registered dietitian about your particular carbohydrate requirements before embarking upon a radical diet. Carbohydrates are a mainstay for brain activity, but as you might imagine, our marvelous machine needs other foods, too.

Nature provides a great number of foods that are great for brain health. The more we steer toward natural foods and away from processed foods, the better off we are. If the food doesn't occur in nature and its name ends in the letter *O*, think twice before eating it. This may seem like a no-brainer, but with the processed food industry in full swing, it might be harder than you think to accomplish. Foods that occur in nature are generally more easily metabolized and better for our brain than ones we invented, and we get better long-term energy from natural foods.[2]

Here are a few of the best brain foods for protection from damaging free radicals and inflammation, cell growth, and mood regulation.

Berries. Berries boost memory function and act as an antioxidant in the brain. The darkest berries are best: blueberry, blackberry, raspberry, and strawberry, in that order. Add cherries for stroke prevention.

Apples. An apple a day, maybe even twice a day, is excellent advice. Apples contain a lot of choline, which helps synapses fire rapidly. Synaptic firing is essential for the brain to talk to itself effectively and make useful connections as we go about our day. It's also true that an apple in the morning will awaken your brain more quickly than a cup of coffee will. Apples and apple juice are excellent before a test or taxing project work. The glucose bump from the natural sugar in apples helps in prefrontal cortex function.[3] Do note that apples are preferable to their juice, though. Most fruit juices have a lot of sugar in them that might not be natural, and even if it is, too much sugar leads to other issues. Also, apple juice lacks the fiber of a real apple. That fiber nicely slows down the uptake of the carbohydrates and delivers glucose to the brain in a more even manner, which is good. A great combination for good carbohydrate uptake is apples with cheese—try it next time you need to work or when your kids need to study.

Turmeric. This is a spice found in curry. It attacks beta-amyloid deposits implicated in Alzheimer's disease. It also has excellent antiinflammatory and antioxidant properties in the brain. Many of the other spices found in curry have a protective effect on the brain, too, including cumin, cloves, and saffron.

Eggs. Eggs are very high in choline, which, as I mentioned earlier, aids synaptic firing in the brain. And yes, you have to eat the yolk. What about the ongoing debate: Does eating a food high in cholesterol translate into more cholesterol in your body? It might, and it might not. We haven't proven either side conclusively. If you have high cholesterol to begin with, work with your doctor to determine the kinds of foods that might reduce it.

Fatty fish. Fish are high in omega-3 fatty acids, which have a positive effect in the brain. These omega-3s support neuronal health and communication. Fatty fish are best, like salmon, sardines, trout, and mackerel.

Oysters, clams, and lamb's liver. All three of these foods are high in the essential brain minerals zinc and iron, and help in memory function.

Cocoa. Yes, chocolate. Dark chocolate boosts endorphins in the brain and reduces the formation of clots, which may help prevent strokes. Note that the darker the chocolate, the better. All things in moderation; a half to one ounce a day (about a two-inch square) of dark chocolate is about right. Be aware that a lot of chocolate is laced with refined sugar—which obviously isn't great.

Nuts and seeds. These are high in vitamin E and help slow cognitive decline; eat about an ounce a day. If you have high blood pressure, eat unsalted nuts. Almonds and walnuts in particular are beneficial to the brain.

Avocados. These are almost as good as blueberries in promoting brain health. They are also high in tyrosine. You want this amino acid in ample doses in your brain. It is an essential building block for dopamine and norepinephrine. It's found in several foods, including seaweed, eggs, low-fat dairy (like cottage cheese), soy, fish, turkey, mustard greens, almonds, and several other foods.

Vegetables. Nature nicely gives us a signal about what vegetables are packed with nutrients by adding deep and vibrant color. Any of the dark leafy greens like spinach and Swiss chard are filled with folate, a B-vitamin the brain uses to make catecholamines. Other folate-rich foods include lentils and asparagus. Tomatoes and peppers carry carotenoids that help counteract free radicals, which damage the mood-protecting fats in the brain. Think about red, orange, and yellow hues in vegetables—and then eat them!

Whole grains. Whole grains such as oatmeal, whole-grain bread, and brown rice are beneficial for blood flow in the brain. That said, there is controversy on grains in the diet. Neurologist David Perlmutter makes the case in his book *Grain Brain* that sugar, whole wheat and white grains, and even an overabundance of carbs are at least in part to blame for the uptick in Alzheimer's disease and other dementia rates. Gluten-free foods are plentiful, and again, consult a dietitian or physician for a discussion about whether this is the right choice for you (it's an ever-changing landscape in the diet world).

Freshly brewed tea, unsweetened. Tea has an antioxidant effect in the body and can increase mood, focus, and memory. Lightly caffeinated tea is fine in moderate amounts and can actually boost mental clearness. Aim for 150 milligrams or less per day, even with coffee. That's about two eight-ounce cups of coffee.

Alcohol. This one doesn't come without controversy, but several key studies point to the beneficial effect of alcohol. Scientific research demonstrates that moderate consumption improves creativity, thinking, reasoning, and memory in aging adults. Moderate is considered two or fewer drinks per night: That's two five-ounce glasses of wine, a total of four ounces of hard liquor, or two beers. Red wine is reported to have a protective aspect, probably due to the resveratrol in the skins of red grapes. It also helps in preventing strokes and mitigating poststroke damage. It's *very* important to note that every person has a different tolerance to alcohol and its sedative effects. It's also very important to note that the line is fine between moderate, beneficial consumption and overconsumption that's detrimental to the brain. If you don't drink alcohol at all, the benefits of it are not so enormous that you should begin now.

Red meat. Of course this one is controversial as well. But red meat is one of the single best sources of quickly absorbed iron, which helps produce the catecholamines that improve mood. People who are iron deficient are 50 percent more likely to become depressed than those with higher iron levels. If you're vegetarian, it's harder to get that same kind of iron; however, beans, dried fruits, and whole grains are all ways to get iron into your diet. Cattle and bison that are fed a strict grass diet produce meat that's higher in omega-3 fatty acids; corn- and grain-fed animals apparently don't give the same benefit. Check your local grocery store, health-food store, or butcher for grass-fed beef and bison. Also, ample doses of the memory-essential nutrient vitamin B-6 are found in animal meats. It can be found in smaller amounts in beans and dark vegetables.

"Bacon." I use "bacon" as a catchall for all the foods we're not supposed to eat but that we love so much that our brain actually experiences pure delight when we put them into our mouth. A healthy existence, in my opinion, isn't about inhibiting yourself so much that you can't ever enjoy anything. Every once in a while, go ahead, splurge. Eat that bacon, or donut, or candy bar—it's a different kind of brain health.

BREATHING FOR YOUR BRAIN, SMELLING FOR YOUR MEMORY

Oxygen is, of course, essential to the brain. Without it, the brain goes dead within a matter of just a few minutes. Big oxygenated blood cells help our brain to do its job well. Exercise is key to brain longevity—to a large extent due to the oxygen we get during it. (We'll talk more about exercise's effect on the brain in chapter 12.) Deep breathing gives us oxygen too; it's an automatic reset back to homeostasis after a threat has passed. Watch next time you feel tense and then relax; the relaxation will most likely come with a heavy breath. We get those deep breaths in—along with that oxygen—on our own throughout the day, and doing so is good for the brain. Yawning is another form of reoxygenating the brain. It isn't always a signal that we need to take a nap, but rather that the brain is yearning for more oxygen.

Additionally, the quality of the air we breathe is very important. Recirculated office air is probably not the best thing to be breathing. Moldy office air has been known to get building occupants sick, and some forms of mold are neurotoxic and will destroy neurons. You may not have the opportunity to test the air in your office building (hopefully, someone else is monitoring that), but for a variety of reasons, it makes sense to step outside a few times a day to get some fresh air. In my all-day workshops, I ask participants to get at least two minutes outside during each break. It's a nice mental health break and the air is hopefully a little cleaner. I've attended conferences where I get so busy speaking and meeting with people that three days later, it occurs to me that I've hardly stepped outside at all. Shame on me. Each day, a few times a day, go outside the office and take deep breaths at least a few times.

Aroma is a powerful tool for our brains. Our olfactory bulbs help to create memory trails that can last the rest of our lives. Scents are linked to the emotional center of our brain, and—as with music—can immediately transport us to a calmer or more invigorated place, and to many places in between. To this day, the smell of Coast deodorant soap transports me to my first day of college, where I used it for the first time. Oncologists sometimes tell patients not to bathe in scents they enjoy while on chemotherapy, so there isn't a memory linking that scent to something negative. However, to soothe a patient's hurting body after chemotherapy, essential oils and aromas are sometimes suggested, and many report that it helps. The importance of aroma isn't lost on spas either. Have you ever walked into a spa and thought it smelled putrid? Probably not. Spas use aroma strategically, to soothe the brain and signal it to relax.

ACTIVATION

- Take breath breaks for a few minutes every few hours; just step outside and take three big breaths. This relieves tension and recalibrates the brain.

- Avoid tobacco smoke in any form (ridiculous to have to say, I know).

- Go to an aromatherapy store and find scents that you love or create a mixture of scents that reminds you of good things. Aromaweb.com and the National Institutes of Health both have resources to help you discover the scents that stimu-late various moods.

- Light incense or candles with a scent.

USING MUSIC TO INCREASE STAMINA AND REDUCE STRESS

There are many times when I am so moved by music that the hair stands up on my arms and neck. I've been moved to cry, laugh, and move my body. There are few things in the universe that are as synchronizing as music—we enjoy it together, and often for the same reasons. Of course, music can be polarizing, too, but in general, it provides us with an opportunity to bond with others, to relax, to emote, or to simply escape for a while.

Music is a great way to distract ourselves from the task at hand and give the brain a break (something I'll explore more in chapter 11). Music can even improve brain performance. Chris Boyd Brewer of Johns Hopkins University writes in his book *Music and Learning*, "Baroque music, such as that composed by Bach, Handel, or Telemann, that is 50 to 80 beats per minute creates an atmosphere of focus that leads students into deep concentration in the alpha brain wave state." Imagine what that can do for us at work.

Music can also be a stimulator and can energize us, allowing us to perform better and longer at tasks we already know how to do. This is especially true of music with a more rapid beat. However, when we're learning something new, music can actually inhibit the processing of new information and slow things down by interfering with short-term memory.[4] So when you're doing something you know, music can pump you up; when you're picking up something new, it will probably be a distractor.

When you are using music to pump up your brain, should it have lyrics or be instrumental? It's a frequently asked question. It's really up to you. There are physicians who say they studied all throughout medical school for rigorous board exams while listening to hard rock, bluegrass, folk, hip-hop, and so on. It becomes a kind of a white noise to them. In my own experience, music without words works best for me. If it does have lyrics, it's better for me if I can't hear or understand the words; otherwise, my brain is working at processing the words.

There are several great books and articles on music and what it does for healing, learning, memorization, attitude, focus, and much more.[5, 6, 7] If you love music and want to learn more about how to use it to improve your stamina, check them out.

ACTIVATION

- Find and listen to music that makes you weep with joy or that makes the hair stand up on the back of your neck with inspiration.

- Check out focusatwill.com, a subscription site that allows you to play music vetted by neuroscientists. The music choices can invigorate you, help you concentrate, slow you down, relax you, and so on. It's one of my favorite sites.

- Find a charge-up song that you can play in the morning on the way to work. Find another song for the way home— something soothing but still invigorating. Or just find a radio station that puts you in the right frame of mind for your circumstance.

- Whatever music you enjoy, think about it as a form of daily nutrition. Use mood-enhancing music as a tool for energy management and increased stamina. It's not an accident that we tend to be in a heightened state of alertness and sometimes threat when we listen to dissonant music or that we feel a sense of calm and sometimes awe when music is consonant and harmonious. Experiment with music, and if you're feeling like you want to delve deeply into music and do something novel at the same time, try learning a new instrument.

CHAPTER 10

Sleep: It's Not a Choice

WE NEED SLEEP TO RECHARGE. It's that simple. Yet sleep is actually more than recharging. When we sleep, we consolidate learning from the day and store information in the brain's memory banks. Without appropriate sleep, our memory, decision making, learning, and executive functioning suffer. Every night, we need to recharge our brains and allow them to download learning from the day so we have the opportunity to grow them even more the next day.

We need approximately four rapid eye movement (REM) cycles a night.[1] Each cycle of REM sleep—also known as slow-wave sleep—lasts about ninety minutes. Add about a half hour of getting into sleep and a half hour of getting out and we're at roughly seven hours, which is close to the amount of sleep the average adult needs: seven to nine hours per night. This is not a weekly average; it's really best to get those hours consistently every night. A small percentage of people actually accomplish all the REM cycles in four or five hours, but these people are few. There are also a few people on the other end of the spectrum who need ten or more hours, but again that's uncommon, and can be a sign of depression. (Check with your doctor if you're either chronically undersleeping or sleeping more than ten hours and still feel tired.)

Despite what most of us know about how we feel when we're sleep deprived, study after study shows that many of us undersleep chronically. The statistics are astounding. About one out of six deadly traffic accidents in the United States is caused by a drowsy driver, according to the American Automobile

Association—and that doesn't include near misses. What's more, the estimated annual cost of sleep-related accidents is about $40 billion.[2] And that's just drivers. What about the toll sleep deprivation takes at home and at work?

The problem with sleep and stress is that the relationship often feels like that between the proverbial chicken and egg. Are we having a hard time getting to and staying asleep because we're stressed out, or are we stressed out because we're not getting enough sleep? It is often difficult to ascertain which one it is. Either way, you need to find a way to solve the root problem; when you do, the other will likely improve, too. I suggest starting with sleep—assuming that if you work first on the quality of your sleep, stress reduction will follow. It rarely makes sense to forgo sleep in order to be a better achiever; you'll seldom, if ever, do better at a task on less sleep.

Once you have a better understanding of what a lack of sleep does to your brain, I bet you'll be more motivated to make it a priority. Understanding just how sleepy most of us are will help, too. We'll explore both before we turn to some tactics for getting better sleep each night.

WHAT A LACK OF SLEEP DOES TO THE BRAIN

The list of ailments brought on and exacerbated by a lack of sleep is long and complex. They include a decaying brain, decreased memory and learning ability, an inefficient immune system, and an inefficient use of fat cells.

The lack of sleep also affects the executive function of the brain, making us cranky and sometimes aggressive. That's because the emotional part of the brain is taking advantage of the fact that the prefrontal cortex is not paying attention to its shenanigans. The emotional brain takes over, and all manner of bad behavior can unfold. When the PFC is tired, we're at the mercy of the emotional threat-detecting architecture of our brain—and that doesn't bode well.

Sleep expert Jessica Payne of the University of Notre Dame and Harvard University[3] says that when we are tired, the following take place:

- Our cortisol levels increase, magnifying our perception of the negative in the environment.

- We have difficulty processing positive attributes in the environment, because the threat network in the brain is on high alert as it tries to help the tired, unalert brain fend off any danger.
- A lack of sleep—such as five hours or less, four nights in a row—can lead to the same lowered mental acuity as drinking a six-pack of beer. When we don't sleep enough, we lose our mental nimbleness.
- Decision making is impaired.
- Insulin regulation is interrupted, which can lead to blood sugar issues and weight gain.
- Memory becomes faulty and, in chronic cases, memories can be completely erased.

Obviously, none of these is good for us in general, but what does it mean in the workplace? We wouldn't put up with people coming to work drunk. Why should we encourage them to come to work chronically tired? Sleep deprivation is an international issue, worth billions of dollars. Think of how much we could save if the entire world's sleep-deprived people got one or two more hours of sleep per night!

Here's the upside. When we do get sleep, we improve overall cognition, creative ability, and mood. As mentioned earlier, we also consolidate memories and fully download the new things we learned during the day. That means that if we're not sleeping, we're not learning, and we can't reinforce and build on all the connections we made during the day.

HOW SLEEPY ARE YOU?

We can get an idea of how tired we are thanks to Dr. Murray Johns and his Epworth Sleepiness Scale. He created the scale at the Epworth Hospital in Australia to establish a baseline for determining how sleepy a person is.[4] You can take the test below and determine where you rate on the scale (thanks to Dr. Johns for the permission). So let's go ahead and see how tired you are. Grab a pen and paper and go for it.

You'll be asked to rate the likelihood of you falling asleep in various situations. Make your determinations based on your life in recent years.

Use the following scale to choose the most appropriate number for each situation:

0 = Would never doze
1 = Slight chance of dozing
2 = Moderate chance of dozing
3 = High chance

Begin scoring for each of the items below:

Sitting and reading

Watching TV

Sitting inactive in a public place (e.g., a theater or a meeting)

As a passenger in a car for an hour without a break

Lying down to rest in the afternoon

Sitting and talking to someone

Sitting quietly after a lunch without alcohol

In a car, while stopped for a few minutes in traffic

SCORING

1–6   You are getting enough sleep

7–8   Your score is average

9+   Seek the advice of a sleep specialist; on average, you will have the same mental sharpness as someone who is legally drunk.

As the scoring indicates, if you're in the 9+ category, now is the time to pay attention to your sleeping habits and take charge (probably with the help of a professional). This could be a lifesaver, not to mention a brain saver, and a relationship saver too.

GETTING MORE AND BETTER ZS

As I've mentioned, the content of your day is downloaded while you sleep.[5] When you take a little more control of that content before you sleep, you may help yourself snooze more peacefully. Think about the time before you go to bed as sacred. It really is one of the few times of day many of us have to ourselves. Be deliberate about your inputs before nodding off, because the content of that input is important to resting well. Some people write in a gratitude journal before they sleep to put them in a positive frame of mind. If you're not prone to keeping a journal, simply thinking about the things you're grateful for is a good way to prime your brain for pleasantness. If that feels too cosmic woo-woo, think about whatever you want, as long as it's positive and feels good. The alternative is thinking about things like nagging work, crisis-filled emails, or concerns about things at home. Ask yourself, "Which would my brain choose if given a choice?"

You can also spend those precious before-bed minutes reflecting on what you learned that day, preferably in writing. Recent research by Francesca Gino and colleagues at Harvard showed that employees who took fifteen minutes at the end of their day to write down lessons from the day performed up to 25 percent better on a test about the content of their jobs than those who worked the extra fifteen minutes.[6] The act of writing is emphasized in the research as a way to help the brain codify what it learned. Gino also found that this practice boosts an individual's confidence and fuels their belief that they can accomplish things; they, in turn, tend to work harder.

You can also plant pleasant thoughts before bed, which may result in more pleasant dreams and better sleep. This one comes from Martin Seligman, who is considered the father of positive psychology. Ironically, Seligman started out studying depression, and one of the interesting things he noted was that people who are chronically depressed report dreams with depressive content. They would even awaken tired, due in part, perhaps, to their restless dreams. Years ago, I was a student of Seligman's, and he once asked our class if we would agree to an experiment exploring the opposite side—positive-content dreams. His hypothesis was that the content of our dreams mirrors the content of our thinking and our life. Keeping in mind how suggestible our brain is, Seligman wondered if we could suggest to our brain something positive before going to sleep, instead of just letting the day's stressors have their way with our dreams. The content could be a grateful reflection on the past day or the hope of a solution to an issue in the upcoming day. He divided us into three groups—one that didn't write anything before bed, one that wrote down something positive that happened during the day for which we were grateful, and one that wrote down a question they were pondering that needed to be solved.

The results were interesting. There were, of course, those who reported not remembering any dreams. What he found in those who did dream, though, was that about 20 percent of each group actually experienced content complementary to their sleep journal assignment. I was assigned to the problem-solving group, and it worked for me. To this day, if I have something to solve, I either write it down before bed or I talk or think about it just before lights-out. The downside is that sometimes I am jolted awake with an angle to an article, and even thoughts in this book have arisen in the middle of the night. Sometimes I get up and write them down so I don't forget and so I signal my brain to release the thought. If you're beckoned awake with a flash of genius, sit up, write it down, and go back to sleep. (Similarly, if you're prone to awakening to thoughts of some task you need to get done, sit up and write it down too. Release the thought from your prefrontal cortex. I've been in that situation, and I've discovered that if I don't write it down, I lay half awake, worrying about whether I'll remember it tomorrow—and then usually forget it anyway.)

Here's one final strategy for inducing quality sleep: Don't let your work intrude too late into the evening. There will always be the occasional times when we have to go above and beyond the call of duty; we've all been up late at night, sending emails to the other side of the world or polishing a presentation as we sit in bed. I've done it too. However, I often hear about executives who do it night after night—I mentioned in the earlier section on parameters how many people admit to being on email after eight o'clock. Some habitually work until eleven or twelve at night, and sometimes later. It would be great if the business world started treating sleep as an absolute nonnegotiable, except in the extreme cases. And it's logical, after all: What boss actually thinks that his or her employees should trade their health for a few last-minute emails that turn into more than an hour of work? Most leaders would want their employees fresh and ready to go, to compose a thoughtful email as opposed to one written in an exhausted haze. They would want you to have great relationships with the people you love, too. You can't have that if your partner is asleep every night while you're slapping on the keyboard into the wee hours, only to get up early the next morning to do it all over again. If that's your habit, I can almost guarantee that your life will change for the positive when you break it. Control that valuable time before you go to bed, and you're likely to sleep a lot more soundly. Your brain will thank you for it.

If you're a chronic insomniac, you already know that for some people, sleeping soundly and naturally through the night is a real struggle. The National Sleep Foundation has a tremendous resource at sleepfoundation.org that can give deeper insights into tools and tactics. Work closely with a sleep physician to determine what could be the underlying cause.

ACTIVATION

- Write in a sleep journal before bed. Do not, however, turn it into a list of things you have to do tomorrow. Do that to-do list earlier in the evening. Instead, write down one new positive thing you learned during your day or something for which you are grateful that day. Allow your brain a chance to consolidate that during your sleep.

- Practice winding down before bed instead of being stimulated until the moment you hit the sheets. Go gently into the last hour of your day. Going from email to sleep is a formula for restlessness. Take a bath or shower, listen to music, read "mind candy" magazines or novels—anything that slows down your brain and readies you for sleep.

- Get emails finished one hour earlier in the evening than you are currently doing. Create a hard-and-fast deadline, only to be violated with exceptions.

- Sleep in a completely dark room. Sleep experts suggest that even a little bit of light through the eyelid can make its way to the retina and trigger wakening chemistry instead of the sleep chemistry you need during the night. Also, get an alarm clock with a red display. Blue and white light have been shown to negatively affect mood the next day—blue being the worst.[7]

- Sleep in a silent room. The brain is constantly scanning the environment, even while we are asleep, so try to give it no reason to pull you awake, such as sound or light. Many people report being lulled to sleep by music or white noise, and that's fine—the sound of a fan or quiet, relaxing music may be an excellent way to induce sleepiness. The trick to staying asleep is to avoid interruptions.

THE POWER OF POWER NAPS

My family knows how important my power naps are to me: If I skip those fifteen-minute naps in the afternoon when I feel like I need them, I suffer, and so does everyone else. But when I get them, they keep me charged up through the rest of the day. You may benefit from power naps, too—evidence shows that napping is good for the brain.

Sara Mednick and Mark Ehrman's book *Take a Nap! Change Your Life* tells us that fifteen to twenty minutes of napping is good for a burst of alertness and improved motor function. Increase it to thirty minutes and you begin to get some memory-consolidation benefit. Sixty to ninety minutes is more of a full-blown nap, but that's where we hit a slow-wave cycle that's imperative for creating new connections in the brain and for decision making.

But, if you don't have the luxury of the sixty-minute nap, here's how experts recommend learning to power nap for a quick refreshing burst. First, if you allow yourself caffeine, drink a cup of coffee just before the nap; the caffeine takes about twenty minutes to kick in. Then set an alarm to go off in twenty minutes; that way you can relax into sleep without being worried about over-sleeping. Now lie down and concentrate on the sound of your breath going in and out of your lungs. As odd as it sounds, some people think about the color of their breath. Hopefully, you'll lull yourself to sleep shortly. Some people awaken from the power nap perky and refreshed, especially if they have used the caffeine method. Others take a little while longer to awaken. Once you're awake, get up right away and begin moving about. That should get the chemistry going to bring about alertness.

So when should you take a nap? For me, it's simple: I don't nap if I'm not tired, and I do nap when I am. There are times when I sit down to read a book and fall asleep, a signal that I must be tired, so I turn it into a quick nap. (Of course, there are times you have to push through sleepiness—you probably shouldn't fall asleep during a meeting or while talking to someone at a party.)

The idea of napping might sound a little taboo to many, but think of it as a brief downtime that makes your up time incredibly productive. In my workshops, I often ask how many attendees take power naps. A few people usually sheepishly raise their hands. One said, "I probably shouldn't say that I do this because I have a colleague in the room." Yet the evidence is clear that those who at least power-nap benefit greatly. Don't ask anyone for permission—just do it. You and your work will benefit, and everyone will wonder why. *Shhhh*. It's your secret!

ACTIVATION

- If you have problems with feeling groggy after a nap and if you allow yourself caffeine, try drinking a cup of coffee or other caffeinated beverage just before lying down for a power nap—caffeine takes about twenty minutes to awaken your brain.

- Lie down or find a comfortable place where you won't be disturbed and where there is low or no light.

- Set an alarm for twenty minutes.

- Concentrate on the sound of your breath coming into your nostrils and filling up your lungs. If you find yourself thinking about work or things to do, come back to the breathing.

- Try to retrain yourself to not think about anything other than your breath.

- Your brain needs to be refreshed and fed and needs time to consolidate all that it is learning.

CHAPTER 11

Give Your Brain a Rest

THE HUMAN BRAIN is like a Labrador retriever. When those sweet, adorable balls of fur finally figure out that you are the alpha dog and caregiver, they trust and love and obey and pretty much do most anything you tell them. Like the Labrador retriever, your brain wants to please and obey you. If you tell it to stay up extra late, it will do everything it can to obey. If you tell it to focus on one task for six hours without a break, it will do what it can to obey. If you tell it to use its impressive reasoning and executive functioning to work for sixty or seventy hours every week, it will try.

Eventually, though, it will fail, because the expectations we have for our brains often aren't realistic. Sometimes, the brain just can't go on any longer, and it goes offline. Think about how hard you go during your day at work. You charge forward all day, but your prefrontal cortex is so exhausted from thinking and negotiating and being "on" that it quietly slips away, and the cranky, emotional center of your brain comes out to play as you walk through the front door of your home. Or maybe you get home and just shut down, sitting on the couch and staring at the wall. Why does this happen? Because the brain really needs to rest. After we put it to work all day, we sometimes don't have anything left for the people we love. The brain just puts itself into a kind of trance, and we can barely utter intelligent syllables unless we're barking something from its emotional center.

If we want stamina, we have to choose when to allow our brain to rest, and we have to make the choice every day. As you know from the previous chapter, sleep is important, but the brain also needs downtime throughout the day, in a form called *awake rest*.

There are many known benefits to giving the brain deliberate rest throughout the day, but here's one of the most convincing: There's evidence that rest can slow the brain's age-related shrinking and can actually increase brain volume in critical areas related to attentional focus, positivity, emotional regulation, and memory storage.[1] It sounds like a laundry list of all the things required for maximum success in a career, and in life in general. When we rest our brains, we improve our chances of boosting those areas, and we don't decay as rapidly. Rest gives us a chance to keep the brain healthy and vibrant into old age.

The bad news is that about one in seven of us past age fifty-five will get some form of dementia, including Alzheimer's disease, arguably one of the scariest and most debilitating mental conditions. Most of us believe that dementia is simply part of the human condition, an inevitable side effect of getting older, but that's not the case. Many forms of dementia are cardiovascular in nature, and we can do something about them (including exercise, which we'll talk about in the next chapter). We don't have to allow many forms of dementia to happen. When they do, it costs billions upon billions of dollars worldwide to manage, billions in lost productivity, and incalculable amounts of heartache for loved ones. There is no panacea to eliminate all of the devastation, but there are things we can start now—and a great place to start is with giving your brain the downtime it needs.

Even if you have a high-pressure job or personal life, you can make choices that help stave off mental decline and help you remain a vibrant, contributing individual well into old age. Think about Grandma Moses, who painted her first painting in her seventies; Fauja Singh, who completed a marathon at the age of one hundred; George Weiss, who at age eighty-four invented the game Dabble, now sold in stores nationwide; and the beloved madam of the cooking shows, Julia Child, who didn't start cooking and creating her famous recipes until she was forty-nine and didn't hit her stride until her sixties. Of course, we would be remiss not to mention the role genetics plays in dementia, because it does have some bearing. However, its role is complicated, and the variances are so great that genes are currently an unreliable predictor. We have to accept that genetic predisposition may increase our individual chances of the brain faltering later in life, but we can't let that stop us from making choices that give us a fighting chance at a robust old age.

The idea that we can grow the brain is exciting, but the rest this requires takes work. Isn't that ironic? Even on the weekends when I'm supposed to be resting, I have to fight off the guilt of having an "unproductive" day. Recently, I was explaining to a friend how utterly lazy I felt when I spent a Saturday reading a novel, napping—a few times—watching mindless TV, and walking the dogs. She said it sounded like the perfect day. Even though I'm convinced by the research on the benefits of rest, I still sometimes have to force myself into that downtime. I've heard many excuses for nonstop work—and I've come up with several of them myself—but the research tells us that awake rest is vital to keeping us from decaying as quickly as we would otherwise. This is definitely a "start small, start now" suggestion—even if you start with short bursts of awake rest, you can start changing your mood, thinking, memory, and behavior for the better. You just have to give yourself permission to be smarter, and part of being smarter means understanding the limits to our brain resources.

Brain rest isn't a guilty pleasure; it's one of the ways we build stamina and energize the brain. Most leaders I've spoken to about this agree that they would prefer a well-rested brain in shorter spurts from employees than a fatigued one that's trying to be productive throughout the day. They are essentially saying they don't want to confuse the appearance of being busy with results.

Awake rest can take many forms, including

- sitting quietly and letting your mind wander
- doing mindfulness exercises (like the raisin exercise I described in chapter 6)
- playing a game like solitaire on the computer for five minutes
- laughing with someone
- listening to music
- meditating

Throughout the rest of the chapter, I'll explain how each of the above can help activate the full power of your brain and protect it against decline. You don't have to do them all, and there are more you can put on the list—anything that allows your brain to take downtime from the rigors of focus. Just pick one or two and try them.

Whatever form of awake rest you decide to do, the evidence is clear: Many of us abuse our brains nonstop. It's so detri*mental*—it takes from our mental capabilities. When positive results come in, who cares if you "wasted" a Saturday resting or took thirty minutes of company time to recharge? Ultimately, getting the proper rest is going to benefit your employer—and you.

REFLECTION AS REST

Do you often go from one meeting to the next, to the next, to the next, without any breaks? When asked, most businesspeople say that the majority of their meetings go over the allotted time, so they're always running late to the next meeting. This doesn't take into consideration the 20 percent of meetings that are unscheduled. In that endless flow of meetings, the PFC doesn't get time to process information or rest for a bit, meaning that your contributions throughout the day will probably deteriorate in quality. And when you're running from meeting to meeting, you don't have time to prepare for the next meeting. Imagine how much more productive most of your meetings would be if each attendee took just five minutes to focus and prepare!

If you are ready to address this problem, I suggest doing a time-out and establishing new rules. If you have control over such things, tell people that from now on, most meetings will last fifty minutes max. That's about as long as we want to attempt to stay actively engaged without a break. You might be surprised at how much more can be accomplished in fifty minutes of focused, energetic collaboration than in a haphazard meeting that runs for two hours. If you don't get everything done in one meeting, call another fifty-minute meeting. You may not be able to change the entire culture of your organization with regard to meeting length, but do what you can to take charge of the meetings you run.

Now, what to do with the ten minutes you've gained back in your hour? Take five minutes after each meeting and write down notes about what you said you would do in the previous meeting and when these items are due. By writing this down, you're dumping these orders out of your prefrontal cortex, leaving your PFC available for more pressing thoughts. In the other five minutes, reflect on the meeting you're about to enter and on what you're going to bring to it. Brilliant things will likely happen if we begin to support each other on getting this reflection time between meetings, and this 50/10 method is just one way to do it. If your day isn't structured around multiple one-hour meetings, adapt the method into something that works for you.

If you make it a priority, you can almost always find snippets of reflection time between work obligations. When you do, you'll find your stamina improved throughout the day; you're giving your brain time to shift into awake-rest mode between periods of active engagement. That can bring a semblance of order and control to your day so that you can accomplish your—and your organization's—goals.

Ten-minute breaks can give you a great refresh at work, but your overall mental strength depends on you taking deeper, non-work-related downtime throughout the day. This should be an everyday practice. When I say this to businesspeople, many of them look at me like a dog trying to understand my words. Disconnect from work every day, while I'm at the office? It doesn't make sense to some people. But during the workweek, try finding reflection time halfway through your morning, during lunchtime, and again halfway through your afternoon. Start with only five minutes each time. Close your office door or leave the building and go on a walk. Turn off your phone, your computer, or any other means of getting ahold of you. Sit for five minutes and just reflect on how the day or week is going. Take stock. You'll slow down the brain and help it consolidate learning. In these moments when you're not taking new inputs, you're helping organize old ones. It gives you time to look back and forth, and calms your threat response; you're establishing certainty through reflection by telling the brain what you expect of it. Once you're up to attempting ten minutes three times a day—only thirty minutes total—you can use some of that time to reflect on work. You can think about what still needs to be taken care of since your last break, and about what's on your plate before your next reflection break.

ACTIVATION

- Hold meetings no longer than fifty minutes and download during the next five minutes all the things you owe from the last meeting. Spend the next five minutes focusing and getting your mind into the next meeting.

- No matter what kind of work you're doing, unless you are fully absorbed and energized while doing the task at hand, work for about fifty minutes and then take a ten-minute reflection break.

- Close your door or go to an empty conference room or go take a walk around the block. No answering phones, pagers, etc. Set some type of alarm for ten minutes. Let your mind wander.

MENTAL WANDERING AS REST

Highly creative people report mental wandering throughout the day. As a matter of fact, the vast majority of us let our minds wander when we're not focused on anything in particular. Neuroscientists say that when our mind wanders, something called the default mode network (DMN) is active.[2, 3] The DMN is an enormous network of many circuits that activates when we've lost our focus and begin to daydream. To illustrate what it is and its benefits, in class I ask participants to go through the raisin exercise with me, very similar to the ECN exercise I described in chapter 6 but this time slightly modified. Remember from the orienting, focused network (ECN) that you were focused on one thing, you were being mindful. The DMN is the opposite; it diverges into various thoughts, usually having nothing to do with the present. A variation of this exercise was used with significant success as early as the late 1980s in chronic pain management and continues to be used today.[4] It's modified here under the assumption I've made that if accessing our DMN could dampen chronic pain, then it might have some benefits outside pain, like changing your mood from frazzled to calm or inducing a sense of creativity.

Recall that the rules are to put a raisin in your mouth for ninety seconds, and to use a timer so you aren't watching the clock. You must not swallow the raisin, and you have to keep it in constant motion. However, this time, the final instruction is different: You can focus on anything you want *except* the raisin. Every time your mind lands on the raisin, you are simply to acknowledge the raisin and then wander elsewhere.

When I do the exercise in a workshop, it is interesting to watch the faces in the room. Only about a quarter of the participants close their eyes, while the rest look around or stare fixedly at something (during the ECN exercise with the raisin, nearly everyone closes their eyes naturally to inhibit stimulation and distraction). When time is up, they explain what they experienced. Was the time long or short? Most say long. Isn't it interesting how a short amount of time becomes very long when we just slow down? There is a huge lesson in just that one point. If you want more time, slow down occasionally. Most say it is difficult to keep the raisin out of their mind. Of course it is, because they have been instructed to *not* pay attention to it. It's like saying to someone, "Don't think of a pink elephant." It is just about impossible not to do so.[5] During the instructions, we acknowledge that mentally landing on the raisin will most likely happen and that when they do they must push their thoughts elsewhere. This exercise is valuable in part because it trains us to acknowledge the "pink elephants" that pop up throughout our day (emails, phone calls, texts, etc.) and move our attention back to something else. It's really difficult not to focus on those distractions, even if we know we're not supposed to.

When the participants describe what they thought about during the ninety seconds (besides occasional thoughts of the raisin), the majority talk about walks on the beach, emails they know are waiting for them, their to-do list, things they should have said in certain situations, and many other thoughts. Nearly all these thoughts have to do with the past or the future; the raisin is in the present, and the participants move away from the present as they try not to think about the raisin. It's the same when the DMN is active in the brain—the mind wanders forward or backward in time but is rarely in the present.

Wandering is fine, but if the content of DMN time turns to negative ruminations, the resultant worry can activate cortisol and lead to a threat response. Some worrying is productive—it's actually an adaptive form of problem solving—but once it gets incessant and we find ourselves going in a circle, never solving the issue we're ruminating on, that's when worry becomes maladaptive and fills us with unnecessary stress.

The DMN is a fine place to be if the content of our thoughts is positive or if we're solving problems. But often when we're in the DMN, we're supposed to be focusing on something else that's right in front of us. We already know that the brain is not equipped to think about more than one thing at the same time, so if your DMN is activated while you're supposed to be doing something else, you're taking cognitive power away from the task at hand.

However, if you're doing mental wandering at an appropriate time, it can improve your innovative abilities and critical thinking.

"Incubation" for Insight

Have you ever gotten stuck working on a project, where you can't create any more useful thoughts? "Stuck" is just a way of describing the times when your prefrontal cortex needs some downtime, needs to be fed, or needs some other kind of input than what we're offering it. One way to get unstuck is by letting your mind wander in a way that can create flashes of insight.

A few forms of distraction are actually good for us and may help reset our brain during a crazy day—even provide insight on the work problem from which we are taking a break.[6] This can be especially true when we've come to an impasse while trying to solve a complex problem. Neuroscientists and other researchers have studied how insight might come about in the brain.[7] Many questions remain, but it seems that there is an interesting calm before the insight storm. It is widely believed that insight happens after an incubatory period where the brain is at rest or wandering, distracted by something completely off the topic at hand. Then, in a burst of electrical gamma-band waves in the brain, a connection is made and the wonderful "aha!" happens. That period of incubation, or downtime, or mental wandering, is critical to the insight happening.

Have you ever had "the answer" just pop into your brain in the shower or while driving? That's an illustration of what happens when we relieve the pressure and allow our minds to wander, completely turning our attention elsewhere. The flash of insight is our brain revealing the answer it has known for a long time. Typically, we have such a heavy cognitive load in our prefrontal cortex that the PFC doesn't notice the answer. When we step away, we give our brain the chance to see what it already knows. We also see this phenomenon when we are talking with someone and trying to come up with the name of a person or a movie or some other tidbit. We press ourselves to remember and then decide it's not important to the conversation. We let it go, and then five minutes later we break into the conversation with the name for which we were searching. It's not an accident. It's how our brain works. Briefly walk away and literally wander when you are stuck so you can recharge your brain and allow it to search for insights and answers without all the pressure.

Here's a series of steps to follow if you intend to go into a mental-wandering state with the hope of getting one of those flashes of insight:

- Find out as much as you can about the problem you're trying to solve.
- Find out what others have done it about it in the past.
- Think of as many new approaches to it as possible.
- Allow yourself to come to an impasse, alone or in debate with another person.
- Remind yourself of the question that you are trying to solve.
- And then go distract yourself. Go let your mind wander.

Playing Games for Rest and Innovation

Games are a form of mental wandering, and they too can give you insight and lower the cortisol that often comes with the anxiety of trying to solve a problem. Think of games not as "goofing off" but as taking your brain for a mental walk. Remember, the brain has a tendency to find insights when we're in a completely relaxed mode and not looking for them. The same can happen when you're doing something completely unrelated to the task at hand, like playing a game. While you may still be fully awake and engaged in the game, you're resting the brain circuitry dedicated to the problem from which you took a break.

Increasingly, we seem to be realizing that the brain enjoys playfulness and rewards us well for it. Silicon Valley is filled with companies that encourage this mental wandering and rest with ping-pong, pool, basketball, and all sorts of other games. This is not by accident. Of course, every company culture is different and busting out into a rousing game of Twister at your office may not go over well. However, do consider working games-as-rest into your day, even if it's just a simple game of solitaire at your desk for ten minutes.

MEDITATION AS REST

General Mills, Target, Aetna, Google, and Green Mountain Coffee are just some of the organizations that are putting their money where their mats are—meditation mats, that is. We've skirted the edges of meditation in our discussions of mindfulness and reflection time, but the true form of meditation seems to cause the more analytical businesspeople among us to go into "cosmic woo-woo" apoplexy. The very word seems to conjure up images of a yogi atop a mountain, in a trance, legs crossed, feeling one with the universe. Okay, that's one form of meditation. But we must acknowledge and learn from a practice that has been around for literally thousands of years; neuroscience is now showing that those who do it on a regular basis have better memory, less dementia, less overall brain shrinkage, increased cortical thickness, and higher reported levels of fulfillment. That's some pretty compelling evidence.

There are many forms of meditation. Some forms focus on breathing, others focus on emptying the mind, others use guided imagery, and still others use mantras. Some forms are appropriate for adults, while others are good for children. The Hawn Foundation's MindUp program (thehawnfoundation.org/mindup), now in more than one thousand kindergarten through eighth-grade schools in Canada and several in the United States, the United Kingdom, China, Australia, and Uganda, reports a reduction in acting out and other maladaptive behaviors associated with attention deficit disorders. MindUp also states that the children's grades are getting better, that class is more civil, and that the kids just like themselves more. Parents report less bad behavior at home, and in many cases, the children are teaching their parents the lessons of mindfulness.

While MindUp has profound results with children, there's an equally dramatic effect on adults who practice it. One child says he taught MindUp techniques to his parents so they wouldn't fight so much—and he says it worked. Teachers who are taught the MindUp curriculum are exposed to the same skills the children are, and reports of less teacher burnout and greater teacher retention are only some of the pluses. MindUp is similar to the raisin activity; each person gets their own rock, and after learning focusing skills by managing outside distractions, they become so familiar with every nook and cranny of their rock that they can pull it from a large pile of similar rocks within seconds. The power of learning this focus affects the person's entire life.

The benefits of meditation are numerous and have been rigorously studied by neuroscientists, psychologists, and sociologists. You can easily research various types of meditation online, and most types are offered in virtually every community in the modern world. But if you don't feel like pursuing that right now, just start small—but start now. Simply find a comfortable spot in your home or your office, turn the lights down low, and turn off anything that might distract you while you're meditating. Sit comfortably with your hands in your lap and your feet in a relaxed position. Concentrate on the sound of your breath for a few minutes without losing focus on it. As with the raisin exercise, keep practicing until you can go for ten minutes or more. It's that simple to get started on your way to an amazing chain of beneficial reactions in the brain.

ACTIVATION

- Practice mindful activities like the raisin exercise to get into the habit of intense focus.

- Meditate just five or ten minutes a day.

Guiding Your Mind

Another great way to begin meditation is guided imagery, a technique you can practice via audio CDs. It is a good way to start since it requires only that you sit quietly with your eyes closed and listen as the voice guides your mind into a quiet place. Jon Kabat-Zinn is considered one of the pioneers of mindfulness and its benefits,[8, 9] and he and many others have guided imagery audio CDs readily available online and at bookstores. Kabat-Zinn's are particularly well known; he began seeing the benefits in his molecular biology laboratory at MIT and now at the Stress Reduction Clinic at the University of Massachusetts. He has elevated the meditation/mindfulness discussion so that now it is included discussions in medicine and with businesspeople, Olympians, and with people in many other walks of life. Much of his work, and that of others, is used in settings worldwide to combat everything from fatigue to depression to pain.

As the name suggests, guided imagery has a visualization component. Often used by skilled athletes[10] and performers, visualization is shown to activate brain regions similar to those activated by the actual activity or sensory input being visualized.[11] It's been shown that merely visualizing a motor skill—such as making the free throw in basketball—can improve a person's ability to perform that skill. Of course, we can't just imagine that we are a rock star and then play guitar overnight. Guided imagery and visualization have to be done with skills we have already practiced and that we have some motor memory of.

But can visualization work beyond motor skills, for the businessperson who's facing myriad complex demands? What should that person visualize? Giving presentations, conducting a meeting, giving a performance review, having a difficult conversation, using empathy and optimism? Difficult conversations are prevalent in everyday work, so let's use that example. Imagining the difficult patches of a hard conversation and how we might approach them is indeed a good way to prepare for the eventuality. Imagining how we might conduct ourselves or direct the conversation to a productive outcome can have a positive effect on our stress levels and put us in a lowered threat state, which in turn can drive more effective behavior and prevent us from getting defensive or shutting down. (It's basically the same technique I suggested earlier, in our discussion of confidence on page 30.)

Remember that your beliefs about stress can have a positive or negative impact on your physiology in stressful situations, which then translate into behaviors. Visualization can help, too, with shifting those beliefs. Take a moment and think through a difficult conversation you had recently. Imagine if you had completely changed your beliefs about how negative that conversation would be and about the person to whom you were talking. What if you imagined the other person in a more gracious and positive light and visualized them working hard to succeed too? Might the outcome have been different? It's worth a try. With practice, you can train yourself, through visualization, to take the higher road during difficult scenarios, and that will hopefully lead to better outcomes. It can lead you to a more positive attitude toward the difficulties in life; the alternative—an automatic, negative approach—is far less productive. Why not give visualization a try and see what happens?

LAUGHTER AND JOY AS REST

Years ago, Herm Albright, a writer for the *Saturday Evening Post*, wrote that "a positive attitude may not cure everything, but it will annoy enough people to make it worth the effort." Earlier, we saw that positive attitude is a neurochemical blend that helps us think more creatively, feel good things about ourselves and others, and broaden our abilities. Many studies have shown that thinking ourselves into a positive state is not only possible but also has a beneficial effect on our abilities. It helps if we kick-start the shift by inducing laughter and joy.

Laughter has so many benefits that an entire encyclopedia could be written on them. It releases chemicals in the brain that allow us to refocus and feel more alert, it dulls pain receptors, it helps improve the immune system and heart health, and it feels just plain good. The "dean of laughter," Robert Provine, a neuroscientist at the University of Maryland, says that along with those health benefits, laughter can also have a significant effect on our mental functions in general.[12] It whisks away the bad mood and anxiety that often come with being stuck on a problem. Laughter pivots our attention away from danger and onto reward. It's an amazing respite from the difficulties of work life.

I keep a laughter file on my computer. When my dad was alive, one of the greatest gifts he gave his children was surfing the Internet for inane videos and jokes and sending them to us. My only rule was nothing political, since I know that things like that increase my cortisol. I shoved Dad's emails into a file, and when I need a mental break, I pull out a few videos or jokes and lighten up my brain. What happens next always stuns me: I can work better and longer just from taking that little laughter break. If you have friends who always make you laugh, keep them on your speed dial for those moments when you need a quick hit of mirth. Researchers have found that we're thirty times more likely to laugh with someone else than when we're alone.[13]

The startling factoid that's often bandied about is that children laugh on average three hundred to four hundred times *per day*, and need no one else around to help. As adults we drop to an average of fifteen times per day. Think about the typical work environment, and levity probably isn't something that comes to mind. Yet, study after study shows that mental breaks that include laughter rejuvenate mental capacity and energy. If you're surrounded by dour curmudgeons for most of the day, sneak away and give yourself at least a chortle or giggle. Find a system that gives you quick access to laughter, and do it often.

Tears can work too, actually. Tears of joy are a very good way to release toxic proteins that may build up in our body as a result of stress. While tears of sorrow will also release those proteins, they're most likely connected to something stress inducing—so go with tears of joy. It doesn't take long to induce tears of joy, as evidenced by those thirty- to sixty-second vignettes on the Foundation for a Better Life's website, at values.com. They're sappy, sure, but they usually focus on doing the right thing and often have an "underdog wins" theme. For most of us, they will cause us to be moved to tears. That feeling always comes with a big sigh of release, which helps us get back to our baseline, unstressed self.

A quick note to my fellow men: We have been socialized not to cry, and certainly not in public. If you've bought into the myth that crying shows weakness, you might reconsider. Certainly, breaking down and bawling at something that happens in the workplace might not be a good idea, but movies, commercials, weddings, funerals, graduations—they're all prime opportunities to show the man you really are. If you feel like it, cry! (If you need to reap the benefits of this cleanser in private, rent *Rudy* or *The Blind Side* or some other appropriately macho sports film that moves you.)

ACTIVATION

- Take time to play games throughout the day, even if it's just playing solitaire for ten minutes.

- Read from your "humor file" of stupid jokes and YouTube videos sent to you.

- Watch touching YouTube channels or videos from sites like www.Values.com.

- Discuss something about which you are curious with an equally curious friend or colleague.

- When faced with a problem, don't leave your desk to tell someone about it (unless it's an emergency) before you have thought of at least two options for a way forward.

- Go gently into your day. Start with morning rituals that put you into a calmer, more positive frame of mind (meditate, listen to music, laugh, play with the kids, walk, pray, love, hot tub). Avoid the abruptness of waking up and running into work (unless you are literally running into work!).

- Talk about the mysteries of life with someone who stimulates you intellectually.

- Go to bed twenty minutes earlier so you can get up earlier. Get up twenty minutes earlier to walk around the block.

- Surround yourself with as many visually and aurally pleasant things as you can as often as you can. You deserve it and your brain does too. Buy a $10 bunch of flowers once a week for your house.

Downtime is critical for the adult human brain. The paradox we have to remember is that with the proper downtime, our uptime can be so much more productive and fulfilling. You now have many suggestions for resting your brain. Try one, some, or all of them, but at least start with a short once-a-day brain break, during which nothing can get into your mind.

So, we've seen that slowing down gives us more stamina. Next, we'll see that speeding up—vigorously moving the body—can boost stamina too, along with the health of our brain cells.

CHAPTER 12

Move to Improve Your Stamina and Your Brain

=====

MANY OF YOU SAY, "I work hard so that I can play hard"; instead, consider flipping it and play hard in order to be able to work hard.

In this discussion of stamina, I've saved the best, most powerful idea for last. According to a huge array of studies, exercise is the single best thing we can do for brain health. Extra oxygen and renewed blood cells help the brain to do its job much better. As Stanford's Director of Longevity and Aging, Laura Carstensen, suggests in her book *A Long Bright Future: Happiness, Health and Financial Security in an Age of Increased Longevity*, there is nothing known to us that can benefit our brain better than exercise. Nothing. In an interview with the magazine of the American Association of Retired Persons,[1] Carstensen suggests that if we could devise a pill that gave our body and brain the benefits of exercise, the yearly billions of dollars of Viagra sales would look like child's play.

One thing before all of the exercise haters skip this chapter: I dislike scheduled and formal physical exercise, too. I've learned how to get it in without a lot of moaning and groaning and I'll tell you what I do. So hang in there! We'll start with mental exercise, which also plays an important role in health, especially when it comes to longevity.

MENTAL EXERCISE

There are many different kinds of brain exercises, including crossword puzzles, word games, and math problems. These are all great for the brain, because they help establish new neural pathways as we work hard to think about things we don't already know. New connections are made when new information is stored. We also "remind" old memories of information we haven't used in a while. As we age, information we used to know naturally fades and becomes dormant, unless we reinforce that information. The mental exercises previously described can help do that.

As we discussed earlier, learning new things is one form of mental exercise. Learning new things changes the shape of our brain. And novelty straddles the fence between physical and mental exercise when you learn martial arts, yoga, dance, or another new sport. For purely mental exercise, think about learning a new language or a new musical instrument, or taking a class on something completely unknown to you just for the pure growth of brain matter.

On top of that, the market is currently burgeoning with "brain growth" software. The neuroscience and learning communities have paired up to collaborate on software that is purported to grow new neural pathways, improve memory, dexterity, hearing, and even driving ability. There are many programs available, and it is hard to say with complete certainty what the results will be. Some of the programs are inexpensive, while others cost $1,000 or more. Though many of the programs were in part developed by neuroscientists, that doesn't guarantee results. There is debate about whether these programs simply improve our skills in one particular game or whether they actually benefit the brain overall. If you do choose to purchase any "brain growth" software, consistency is the key to drawing benefit from it (as it is with learning any new skill). I can't recommend any one in particular. Go at your own peril, but have fun and be consistent for the best results.

ACTIVATION

- Remember the lessons from novelty and learning something new that is mentally challenging, like a language, or physically new, like martial arts.

- Work on difficult problems and calculations.

- Analyzing information to come to a new conclusion is excellent for the brain.

- Do word and math games. Relearn the multiplication tables with your kids.

- Invest in brain game software.

PHYSICAL EXERCISE

Then there's physical exercise, which is one of the single greatest predictors of brain health as we age. One of the most substantial benefits of exercise, other than feeling good, is the release of a chemical—brain-derived neurotrophic factor, or BDNF—that actually helps our brain to grow, allowing us to slow down the approximate 0.5 percent annual brain shrinkage we experience after the age of forty. Dr. John Ratey, of Harvard, dubbed BDNF "Miracle-Gro for the brain,"[2] and it's released when we exercise. It literally plumps up the areas of the brain that store memories, helps repair damaged brain cells, and allows the connections in the brain to work better. With BDNF helping it along, the brain doesn't have to decay as rapidly in old age—but we have to exercise both mentally and physically.

Recent research has shown that to get the benefit of BDNF, we need about 150 minutes a week of aerobic exercise. Jumping up and down or taking Zumba or kickboxing classes are enough exertion to release BDNF, but if those aren't in the cards for you, walking vigorously does the trick too. Whatever you do, just get your heart rate up to the point that you notice a little huff and puff.

People usually fall into one of four camps when it comes to physical exercise: those who love it and do it nearly every day and get grouchy if they can't; those who sort of enjoy it and get to the gym or purposefully exercise at least three times a week; those who don't like it much but know it's critical to health and well-being, so they get a workout buddy or personal trainer; and those who hate it and don't do it. Where do you put yourself? Regardless of the category you're in, we all must get exercise somehow, some way. Our ancestors didn't have to be told to do it; they walked miles and miles to find shelter and food. Now that those are more readily available, we might walk a few feet around the office or from the kitchen to the couch.

I never responded well to being harped on to exercise, and it felt like everyday exercisers were a different species from me. I still work to do it vigorously most days of the week. The key, of course, is to start small, and start now. If you just start, exercise will likely become more like brushing your teeth than scaling Mount Everest. Sometimes an accountability pal and a little perspective get us going faster than anything else.

Plenty of people decide to take charge of their health at some point in their lives, and many have different reasons for doing it. I exercise mainly for my brain, but my body benefits too. Others coax themselves into the gym because they want their body to look better or be healthier. No matter what drives us to work out, we can't always know all the benefits we and the people around us will reap. A client of mine named Mark decided to take the "start small, start now" challenge and start exercising after he had an eye-opening epiphany in my leadership course. According to Mark, everyone around him is benefiting from his decision. He lost seventy pounds, and his before-and-after pictures are astounding. As wonderful as that is, that's only one of the gifts he is receiving. His wife and friends are in the challenge with him and getting healthier along with him, walking daily and eating better. And, as Mark says, "First, I am healthier. Beyond that, I feel a deep sense of accomplishment and control . . . and pride. I know that I will be around longer than likely would have been the case otherwise, and I have rolled back the clock." As for his work as a vice president of a Fortune 50 company: "Whether reality or just my perception, new and longtime colleagues seem to view me in a different light. Certainly, I have more confidence."

The brain rewards us with amazing positive chemistry when we exercise, leading to outward benefits like better appearance and inward benefits like less depression and anxiety,[3] confidence, control, and a better overall operating system.[4]

The benefits of exercise are indisputable. It's about paying slightly more attention to our body and the brain inside it. When they feel the difference, so do our friends, family, and colleagues. We also get a chance to stay around a whole lot longer as productive, contributing individuals. You don't have to be Olympic caliber or own amazing gym clothes and shoes; you just have to get going now before it's too late for your brain. Start moving to exercise your brain today. Forget about trying to like it for now; that may never come. But exercise, no matter what.

ACTIVATION

- Aerobic exercise for twenty to thirty minutes, five days a week—shoot for 150 minutes weekly.

- Buy a pedometer and go for a target of 10,000 steps per day. On average the number of steps in a mile is about 2,000. Five miles of walking throughout the day is a hefty target, and wearing a pedometer can help you get closer. There are some days when I look down (especially as I am writing) and my pedometer says 1,500 steps and it's four in the afternoon. Eek! My dogs get a very long and vigorous walk at that point.

- Do things that get you moving but that you also enjoy, like gardening or dancing.

- Read Chris Crowley and Henry Lodge's *Younger Next Year.*

Stamina is one of the most exciting words in our vocabulary. It helps us keep forward motion, no matter how small or large the energy we're expending is. When we feel in control of our lives on a day-to-day basis, we are likely to gain more energy as we find more of our time focused on the things that inspire us. Some of that refound energy can be used to get more energy—a body (and brain) in motion stays in motion. And when we have more energy, we are more productive, more emotionally stable, more fulfilled in our lives, more present for what matters.

Some of that energy can also be applied to one of the most profound gifts of the human brain: leading a life of significance and leaving a legacy through our connections and interactions with others. The ripple effect we create with a healthy, long-lasting brain can be staggering—and all you have to do is decide to participate.

4

Finding Significance

CHAPTER 13

Significance Through Connectedness: Mother Nature's Bonding Glue

I WAS PEOPLE-WATCHING, as I so often do in airports, when the mom sitting next to me said to her teenage son, "Josh, you have five more minutes and then the iPhone goes in my purse." Of course, Josh whined a bit without looking up from his phone. As if a cuckoo clock had chimed, five minutes later, Mom told Josh to hand over the phone. "Oh, Mom! Just one more minute," he begged.

"Nope, Josh, you know the deal."

He handed over the phone. I was curious to see what "the deal" was, so I watched. Apparently the deal was that he simply sit in the waiting area and observe his surroundings. He did so for about fifteen minutes. He got into a side conversation with his mom about the people passing by. When he excused himself to go to the restroom, I took that opportunity to get into conversation with the mom and, apologizing for eavesdropping, told her I am a student of human behavior. I told her I couldn't help but notice the scene between her and her son. She told me, "There are very few times where I lay down the law with my son—but unburying him in technology is one of them. I told him he would learn more about people and life in ten minutes of watching people in an airport than he would in his phone. I don't want him to miss the sheer pleasure of just watching. He proves me right every time."

What an incredible gift she is giving her son, showing him the value of being present where he is, connecting with and learning about others, not buried in his phone, looking to escape now. It's unlikely that he'd find the same sense of significance in his interactions with his phone. Significance is something we all desire—the ability to connect with others and to work with them to influence the world around us in a positive way.

Why is watching people at airports or observing children at play so engrossing? It's because we're inherently interested in others in our species; we're fascinated by each other. Unlike the rest of our organs, the human brain is social.[1] For instance, we have that ability to "mentalize"—to think about what other people are thinking about—and we have dedicated neuro architecture that activates when we think about other people. Without each other, it is doubtful that we would have survived the perils of the natural world, because we are ultimately very physically weak. As babies, we can't run from our prey or feed ourselves. A woman would need to gestate a fetus for approximately twenty months to get it to that point. And still, we would need each other to be able to reach adulthood, because our brain doesn't become fully grown until our mid-twenties.

The brain is in a constant flux of neurochemical change and electrical impulse; it's an organ growing and shifting and reshaping as it interacts with other humans. That interplay creates who we are. Ponder this: Each interaction we have with another human being literally changes who we are—even if the change is small. Put in those terms, we can feel the real gravity of understanding our own significance and helping illuminate it in others.

I sometimes catch myself bewitched with others in airports and hotel lounges, as if I had never seen another human being before. Billions of people watch others push the boundaries of our species' physical ability in the Olympics. But what most will say is even more fascinating is the story behind the athlete's struggle. The significance of the competition is not the competition itself; it is the journey that person took to get there. We want to go on the journey vicariously; we want to feel connected to those athletes. So we watch, and we discuss, and we cheer or even cry. These are the very same things we can do in our everyday life with our colleagues and family.

We are happier and more fulfilled when we're developing a sense of significance through our connections with others, and when we're creating feelings of significance in others. Let's explore how we can do both of those things.

CREATING SIGNIFICANCE FOR OTHERS

In social science, 1 + 1 = 3. There is me + there is you = there is us. Each time we add another person to the equation a whole set of new interactions takes place, and therein is our ability to create substantial significance in our own and others' worlds.

British anthropologist Robin Dunbar is famous for his "Dunbar's number," a measurement that puts an important perspective on this social multiplication and gives perspective to how much impact we can have in the world with relatively few interactions. Dunbar's number suggests how many people we can truly trust, in general.[2] Essentially, the capacity of the real estate in our brain to truly trust and know others deeply is maxed out at about 150 people. But, it's the ripple effect of knowing those people and then the people who they know and then the people who they know that really tells us about the significance we can create. By the time we get just a few layers away from our 150 intimates, we can have an impact on literally millions of people.

The social media site LinkedIn illustrates something like Dunbar's number by showing us how many people we are connected to who are connected to others we don't know, and how that third tier is connected to even more. According to LinkedIn, when I check, I am "connected" to 20,230,808 people. If even a fraction of that is true, we have some exciting things we can do. Plus, our brain is going to allow us to do that if we pay attention to the health of our brain, as is suggested throughout the book.

How do we use that ripple effect to create significance for others? Humans can do that, but there is a notion that in order to have any great impact on others, we need to have a big title in our company. Yet, as scientist Margaret Mead said, "Never believe that a few caring people can't change the world. For, indeed, that's all who ever have." Maybe your goal is not to change the world, but do you want to at least have a significant impact on your work and your family? If so, it requires awareness of who you are and how you go about interacting every day; you have to live life by design and not by default.

What conversations of significance are you starting in your organization? The corporate superstars of our time all started important conversations. People like Steve Jobs, Meg Whitman, Mary Kay Ash, Bill Gates, and Warren Buffett. And then there are people like the rest of us—we can start conversations of significance, too. Why not? Consider Nancy Brinker, who promised her sister who died at age thirty-six from breast cancer that she would help create awareness so that something could be done about this devastating disease. That sister was Susan G. Komen, and today the foundation of the same name is one of the most respected in the world, having raised over $1.5 billion for breast cancer research.

Then there are the everyday people in nearly every company who start conversations that will make the place better, more profitable, more important. Back in 1984, before smoke-free environments were in vogue, one of the nonsmokers at the TV station I worked at pitched the idea of having a place for the smokers—and there were a considerable number in 1984—to go for cigarettes. Their smoke would be ventilated and wouldn't disturb the lungs of nonsmokers. A smokers' lounge was born, and the rest of us breathed a sigh of relief. Your company has ordinary employees who start significant conversations, too. Maybe it's you. Those conversations give the company soul, just like they give individuals and the rest of the world the same thing.

The interesting thing is that very few significant things get accomplished without conversation and collaboration. The smokers' lounge at my old station certainly didn't. Our own significance usually comes about because of—not in spite of—others. People who have an impact and who create significance are almost always able to create, nurture, and maintain relationships—working through and with others. Relatively few of us create an impact and significance by going it alone. And, why would we? We're wired to work together.

Creating significance is the crowning achievement in our lives. Let's now look at another ingredient that's consistently present when significance is created: trust.

BUILDING CONNECTEDNESS BY BUILDING TRUST

When asked about the requirements for any successful relationship, whether it's personal, political, or business, people most often say the most important factor is trust. If you've ever lost trust in an important relationship, you understand the profound negative effect that can have. Of course there's a similarly profound positive impact when trust is present in a relationship.

An employee's entire career is predicated on whether they can be trusted to get the job done. When that trust has been violated, the employee is passed over for promotions, gets demoted, or may even be fired. Look at your own company and think about the currency of trust there. Who do you resonate with most in your organization? It's doubtful it will be someone with whom you have no trust. And don't we do more and reach further for those we trust?

The creation of trust doesn't have to be an accident; in fact, it rarely comes about without some deliberate effort. But we often find ourselves too busy to pay attention to the fabric of the relationships in our personal life and at work. Then one day we look up and we wonder why things aren't working. It's likely the lack of nurturing trust.

Trust is difficult to build, easy to lose, and really challenging to get back once violated. Yet it's the primary glue between all of us, so it pays to understand it and make it a chief area of focus in our lives. How do we get it, keep it, and use it? Let's look at the brain science of trust for some clues.

The Brain Science of Trust

Chemically it begins with the brain hormone oxytocin, which is getting a lot of play lately—primarily for its role in trust. Paul Zak, a neuroeconomist at the University of Pennsylvania, conducted an experiment in which he took fMRI scans of subjects in stressful social situations.[3, 4] He found that we have a threat reaction in the amygdalae when we first meet someone we don't know. That's easy to understand when you notice that most of us behave in slightly "tighter" and more controlled ways when we meet someone new. We're on our best behavior, because we want to be judged well in that setting. We have an even larger threat response when we are met with an entire group of people we don't know. Think about the last time you walked into a party full of unfamiliar faces. Did you look around and try to find the person who invited you? It typically feels awkward if we can't find them, so we might head over to the bar, where everyone else is who doesn't know someone. As I mentioned earlier in the book, Paul Zak also created an oxytocin nasal spray, gave it to test subjects, and put them through the same threat tests. He discovered that oxytocin wipes out nearly all threat response in the brain. It creates a safe, trusting feeling.

This makes sense when we consider that oxytocin increases as we are finding our mate. It's that love-at-first-sight hormone, that tingly, excited, can't-stop-thinking-about-the-other-person feeling. It seems to magnify the positive and create a bonding feeling. It allows us to act overly interested in the fact that our companion went shopping for socks today. Oxytocin typically tapers off as the relationship continues; at that point, with this new understanding of the bonding hormone, we can activate trust deliberately.

Building Trust and Bonding Actively

It takes some work to build trust. But the world gets to benefit in significant ways when we actually do that hard work. As we build trust and increase our oxytocin levels, the effect spreads, because emotions are contagious.[5]

Here are some things that we know help us trust each other (and that increase oxytocin):

- Reliability and/or credibility
- Generosity and benevolence
- Collaboration
- Loving/liking relationships
- Laughter (particularly infants' laughter)[6]
- A pat on the shoulder—literally
- Knowing the trust equation: consistent behavior over time (credibility) + benevolence = trust[7]

Let's take a look at how some of these simple elements of trust were nurtured in just one day at one of the world's most well-respected companies. As you read, I invite you to extrapolate ways that you might do something like this in your own company. It doesn't have to be a huge production, but it does require some effort, like any good relationship.

Many companies have matching plans whereby they match a portion or all of what an employee gives to a charity of their choice. One group of business-people learned how significance becomes a ripple effect when there is trust. On the day I am about to describe, this group encountered all of the elements of trust. Let's learn from their experience.

Here's the setup: A group of 150 high-level executives were in a team-build-ing exercise intended to raise money for charity. The executives broke up into various clans with different projects they had to complete by the end of the day. One clan had to take everyday household appliances, deconstruct them, and turn them into works of art. Another clan got to work with fashion designers to create garments for a runway show; another created a gourmet meal with a professional chef as the tutor. There were furniture-making and jewelry-making teams, and one team made its own beautifully scented soaps to be sold in gift baskets. It all seems kind of silly until you realize that these are the top 5 per-cent of leaders of one of the world's most respected companies, and they were very serious about their fun, which turned out to create intense trust between group members. At the end of the day, there was a big dinner, and a professional auctioneer came and sold off all the goods the teams had made. They raised $56,000 in one night, matched 100 percent by the company. That money went to the Philippines as that country was battling the aftermath of the horrible tsunami of November 2013.

Let's look at what this day did for the participants in terms of trust. At its highest level and purpose, it connected a globally diverse group of corporate leaders and united them around a higher purpose, beyond the spreadsheets and client calls of their everyday jobs. It bonded individuals who had never worked together before; many had never even met before. They *had* to trust each other; otherwise, they would never complete their tasks by the end of the day. Most of the individuals had no experience with any of the creative endeavors. They were all beginners to some degree, all in it together. There was a lot of uncertainty going on that day. The ones who did have experience with the particular skill had to assert their skills in a group of people who were used to doing the asserting. They had to build quick relationships of trust to prevent things from devolving into a status battle.

One of the benefits of trust is transparency and honesty. When I watched these people in their quickly built but nevertheless trusting relationships, I saw them owning up to what they could and could not do. They were transparent and vulnerable. They asked for help, as opposed to sweeping their vulnerabilities under the rug. They were also willing to tell the truth to each other. When something didn't work or looked bad, they were able to say it outright because they had built a safe, trusting relationship. Without trust, transparency and vulnerability feel too scary, and so we usually mask our inabilities and don't bother getting help. Without trust, we often don't speak up when we see something wrong. Honesty takes a backseat in order to calm the threat of a lack of trust, and so we don't say anything. That's not what happened in these teams.

Participants laughed throughout the day as they freed themselves of the self-consciousness that often comes with perfectionism. Laughter is a nice release of positive hormones, including oxytocin, and helps bring down self-consciousness.

These people also really liked each other. Collaboration with people you like is yet another oxytocin enhancer, which we'll discuss in more detail in the final chapter of this book. Have you ever worked on a team of people who you genuinely liked? Isn't the experience amazing, and don't you often produce excellence? Contrast that with teams where you don't know each other well enough to like each other. The only thing you can judge is the person's latest performance, and when that falls apart, the relationship falls apart because there's nothing else holding it together.

And finally, on that one day, there were more high-fives, hugs, and slapping of backs than most people will receive in an entire year. Each of those releases oxytocin as well. In fact, one study shows that basketball teams that touch more in games with high-fives, back slaps, and other celebratory touches perform better in the long run.[8]

The nice thing about trust is that we can ride on events like these for a long while, and we often have smaller versions of events like these in our lives—tough projects we tackle together, bonding experiences, and the like. We don't have to have enormous daylong activities to keep the trust going. We can do small things daily that build generosity, liking, laughter, and collaboration.

At Centura Health, a large hospital system, administrative teams begin every meeting with a reflection on something good in their world. It could be something interesting that happened to an individual, a profound quote, or a parable. This happens at every meeting. It's a positive thing, and it only takes three minutes. It sets the tone of respect, positivity, and trust. These are executives and physicians with MDs, PhDs, and MBAs. They don't roll their eyes at these small three-minute pebbles of significance. It builds trust, so they do it.

On a personal note, if you're having a low point in your relationship with your significant other, you might try something like this. Get out photos from a trip the two of you both enjoyed. You don't have to say anything. Flip through the pictures together and watch what happens. "Oh yeah! Remember that hike when we found that..." Some of the unsafe feelings that are created during times of low or no trust dissipate. Somehow, it loosens our forgiveness lever and we find it easier to say something like "I'm sorry I've been..." We bump up that bonding hormone oxytocin, and then a civil conversation might actually take place.

Relationships can be complicated, but we can create an impact and help others to do so when trust is present. It's the beginning.

ACTIVATION

- Start small: Creating significance doesn't have to be about winning the Nobel Prize. Tip an extra dollar at a restaurant where you've gotten great service, just because. The ripple begins.

- Randomly say thanks to a respected colleague. Tell them why they are valuable to the team. Imagine if out of the blue a colleague came up to you and said, "I haven't said this to you before, but I get such a great charge out of working with you. You're a great model and inspiration. That's all. Thanks."

- Take a colleague to coffee just to catch up. Avoid talking business for the time being. Bond.

- High-five. Bump knuckles. Shake hands. Make sure these connections are appropriate, but do connect with people.

- Understand how others perceive your behavior. What they see from you consistently is what they will come to trust.

- Laugh. Lightness doesn't indicate a lack of serious thinking.

Trust is critical to doing business, mending relationships, building a better world, and creating significance. Awareness of how we elicit trust in others gets us one step closer to significance. Our next step is understanding our personal strengths and the personal weaknesses that could help or hinder our trust-making ability.

BUILDING CONNECTEDNESS THROUGH ACTIVE-CONSTRUCTIVE COMMUNICATION

Shelly Gable, a professor of psychology and brain sciences at UC Santa Barbara, and her colleagues are credited with research showing that the best predictor of a couple's relationship is how they celebrate the good times as opposed to how they mend the bad times.[9] This is an excellent principle to adopt in business. It's all about staying positive, but this can be a challenge, especially when we're focused on our own needs. But when we emphasize the good, it's completely disarming. It works.

Gable explores what makes relationships better. Her techniques have flown through positive psychology circles and are now in the hands of all of us. I've found that one of these techniques works especially well when we use it with people who are difficult to deal with. It is called active-constructive responding (ACR).

People often tell us about victories, triumphs, and smaller good things that happened to them recently. How we respond to them can either build the relationship or undermine it. There are four basic ways of responding, only one of which builds the relationship: a response that's *active* and *constructive*. Take the time to ask about good things that happened to the person recently and then ask at least three questions that follow up on the good event. Then listen to the responses.

Here is an example of Gable's model and the four types of responses. We'll start with the one you want to practice: the active-constructive response.

Active-Constructive

> JANE: I am so excited! Our biggest client just signed off on a
> major contract I sold them!
> DAVID: That is so cool! I know you've been working your tail
> off on that one. How did they tell you?

Everything that comes from David's simple response is focused on Jane and her good news. David matches her enthusiasm, at least to some degree. This would actually work with bad news as well. As long as the focus is on the speaker and somewhat matches their emotion, that's the right direction. My additional rule to Gable's model is to ask at least three questions during the course of the conversation, or make constructive statements about the speaker's news.

What would it sound like if David didn't stay in the conversation and didn't match Jane's emotions? It might sound like this:

Passive-Constructive

> JANE: I am so excited! Our biggest client just signed off on a
> major contract I sold them!
> DAVID: That's great news.

No emotional matching, no follow-up. Few things say we're finished talking about your news more quickly than this style. At least it's passively positive. If you get in the habit of meeting other people's news this way, they'll tend to stop sharing with you, or they'll anticipate your low celebratory reaction by delivering the news as "Oh, by the way, that project I told you about closed." When that happens, you miss out on big opportunities to deepen the relationship.

But, it can actually be worse. Here's Jane's news met by an actively-destructive response.

Active-Destructive

> JANE: I am so excited! Our biggest client just signed off on a major contract I sold them!
>
> DAVID: You know, all that means is that you'll be gone a lot more, and with the track record of your company, you're probably not going to see any more pay from it. You'd be better off without all the crap that contract is going to bring.

Ouch! This one not only misses the idea of emotionally matching Jane's news—it is negative as opposed to positive—it rips down her news and offers advice she's not looking for. Who wants or needs advice about good news when they are looking for celebration? It's almost as if someone told David that they just won a million dollars in the lottery and the only thing David can think to say is "Taxes are going to be big on that." Way to go, David, blow the high.

But this still isn't the worst way to respond. Check this out.

Passive-Destructive

> JANE: I am so excited! Our biggest client just signed off on a major contract I sold them!
>
> DAVID: Oh, hey, I'm going over to Mark's house for a beer.

This is the ultimate in ignoring—a major distance is created in the relationship. Apathy can lead to contempt and then the relationship is in a very bad spot.

People are people wherever they go and want and crave the attention you give them, especially when they alert you through the tone of their voice that they have major news and need you to either celebrate with them or just be a good listener.

No Time to Be Kind—I'm Too Busy

I've gotten a few objections to ACR in workshops, and I'd like to address them. One is "What if I'm too tired or busy to engage in bantering?"

If you're having problems being available, you're not alone. Many of us are entirely spent during the workday and certainly by the time we get to the end of it, and that is unfortunate. It's a sad fact that we are often least available to our colleagues and those most important to us at home because we haven't managed our energy well throughout the day.

When we find ourselves focused on our own needs, it's difficult to be a part of someone else's needs, and our ability to create significance becomes just about nil. We may need to rethink the way we live life if that's consistently the case. It's so important to be available for important relationships at work and those precious moments at home. You might revisit part 3 of this book, on stamina, to determine if you're taking care of your brain in the way it needs. Until then, sometimes we have to do what we have to do to maintain an important relationship: Use ACR even when we don't feel like it. We owe it to the people we respect at work and those we love at home. So it's important to reiterate that these principles apply when we are at work interacting with colleagues. Push away from the computer, listen, and be interested. The few extra minutes it might take to engage is paid back many times over in goodwill, trust, and connectedness.

I heard poet David Whyte speak one time at a success forum. He wrote a magnificent tome about the soul of the corporation called *The Heart Aroused: Poetry and the Preservation of the Soul in Corporate America*. He was talking about how men and women communicate differently. He said women will want to pick up on the last conversation and men will be stumped because they believe the conversation was done and over with. He said something profound after that—something to the effect that men need to understand something about conversations. The relationship is *about* the conversation, and when the conversation is over, the relationship is over. ACR keeps us in the conversation.

Another frequently mentioned obstacle to engaging in ACR is "What if you aren't as excited about the news as the one offering it up?" What if your significant other comes home with bad news, and you just don't think it's that bad, and they're making a bigger deal out of it than is necessary? If that happens, turn the tables and imagine that you got some big piece of news, and you're met with someone's negative opinion about it. You become deflated, and the entire conversation derails. Again, relationships—business or personal—require work. Try choosing to actively listen and care, even if your caring is a little bit less than the news bearer, and see what happens in all of your relationships.

Here's a warning about ACR: If you are not the kind of communicator who usually shows interest in your partner or other people in your life, then ACR is going to seem completely foreign coming from you. In one workshop I held, the overnight homework was to try ACR at home and report back the next morning. One man reported that his wife thought he was having an affair! He didn't warn her about the tactic he learned in class and all of a sudden he was acting more interested than usual. So warn people; tell them you've learned a new technique and discovered that you might not be participating in conversations as actively as you could, and that you're going to try new techniques.

ACR works, and if you're not currently doing some form of it in your business and personal relationships, start: It will change them positively in considerable ways. Give it a try and get on the bandwagon of making others feel significant.

ACTIVATION

- Practice ACR when a colleague casually tells you about something good, like how their weekend was, or when they describe the difficulty of something, like getting a project done.

- If you have children, practice ACR on them.

- When you get good at ACR, notice or even journal about the reaction you get from the recipient. Notice if you feel more connected to them.

Have you ever thought, really thought, about the legacy you will leave? Steven Covey had us think about our lives with the end in mind; what will people say about us at our funeral?[10] That is one way to think about the significance we want to experience in our own lives and the significance we want to help create in others' lives.

In order to achieve this wonderful goal, though, we have to get a grip on our ego.

CHAPTER 14

The Ego: Choosing Your Best You

IF YOU'VE EVER WATCHED NBC's *The Voice* and listened to the judges give critical feedback to someone who didn't get selected to continue on the show, you've seen some of the most elegant ego management anywhere. When the contestant is finished, the judges always ask him or her about who they are and what their interests are. They identify where the contestant performed beautifully, and then with honesty and kindness, they tell them where they could bolster their skills for next time. They often connect with the contestant by telling them of some of their own failures along the way. Their handling of the situation likely leaves a significant and positive impact on people who might otherwise have felt completely rejected.

Wouldn't it be great if all our interactions were like that? If we could all choose to be our best in each interaction? Although we often feel that we are driven to bad behavior by situations and other people, we do have a choice. And it starts with understanding our own ego and the egos of the people around us. That's how you choose your best you. For those who groan thinking this is the latest idea on "being nice" in order to give feedback and that you don't have the time to be anything but "*brutally* honest," think about it this way. Your colleagues and employees are assets. If you kick your assets enough, they will become lame and can't or won't support you eventually. However, if your intent is to move them forward somehow—to teach them—they become a better, more skilled asset.

Ego is the Latin word for self. It's the sense we have of ourselves. When I hear someone remark that "We need to get the ego out of the room when we're making this decision," or something of the sort, I think to myself, "Then we would all be dead." Ego is something we carry with us all of our life.

Managing your own ego is essential for making a significant positive impact at work and at home, and for building connectedness. We have a choice to make during nearly every conversation we have, and that choice makes an enormous difference in our trust levels and our overall success with others. When we understand how we show up in interactions—and it's different from situation to situation—we can have a say in our connectedness to others, and in the trust that we build. The more connected we feel to others, the more positive impact we can have in the situation—even when delivering bad news.

Trust is affected by the state of our ego. If we sense that someone is self-centered—has only their best interests at heart—that feels threatening, and we'll probably trust them less. That's why paying attention to the ego is critical in building trust.

To begin to understand how we show up in each daily interaction, here are a few things to keep in mind:

- What you believe about yourself predicts your behavior, at least to some extent.
- People around you are a better barometer of your impact on them than you are, so listen to them. Believe what they say.
- The one thing all of your bad relationships have in common is you. (A humbling thought, isn't it?)
- You cannot change anyone, and you cannot be responsible for others' bad behavior. However, *you* can adapt to them to be successful.
- You can be responsible for your own bad behavior.

When we talk about ego, we're usually talking about its strength and how we express it. We want ego strength, not weakness, but understanding how to achieve that requires us to explore the various facets of ego and how we can move from one ego position to another throughout the day.

EGO STRENGTH AND EGO EXPRESSION

The chart below is overly simplified in order to make the point; the nuances of ego are far more complex. It won't answer everything about ourselves, but it explains a lot. Try to resist pigeonholing yourself or others as we go through the chart. We've all been in all of the boxes, and sometimes all of them in one day.

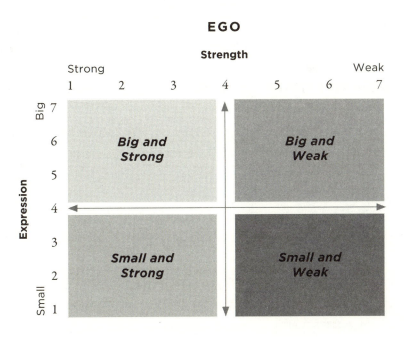

Figure 2

Expressing Ourselves

On the left side of the chart is the expression axis. Think about how you feel and act in a slightly threatening environment, like a party or workshop where you know no one, or when you meet an individual for the first time. We tend to narrow our behaviors when we feel threatened, while our behavior becomes more exaggerated when we feel safe. Think about it; we become more expressive and animated with those we know, as well as sometimes ruder and more thoughtless.

Your level of expressiveness is one of the first things people note when you walk into a social situation. Those of us on the less expressive (small) side of the chart might look around and wait for others to come to us, or, in a classroom environment, we might nest, putting our belongings neatly on the table and letting others approach. The less expressive are fully able to carry on a conversation, but we're typically not the driver of it. That's going to be the lower expressive side of the chart, rated from one to three. In Jungian terms, you would be more introverted.

Those of us on the more expressive (big) side of the chart have a tendency to be more outward in our expression. We walk into a party or a workshop full of people we don't know and begin to introduce ourselves all around. The sevens on the chart are the ones who are comfortable wearing the T-shirt that says, "I'm talking and I can't shut up!" The fives and sixes are a little less gregarious, but expressive all the same.

If you find yourself in the "It completely depends on the situation" category—a four—note whether you have a tendency, even a slight one, to be on the more expressive or less expressive side of the chart. This isn't scientific; it's just a way for you to think about how you come across in a social situation.

There's no judgment good or bad about expressiveness. As with most behaviors, there are pluses and minuses. On the plus side, less-expressive people are often excellent listeners and let their actions speak for them. They often passively participate by laughing at the jokes but not being the joke-teller. Expressive people are gregarious, keep a conversation going, and are often described as fun. We often know what they are thinking, because they tell us.

On the downside, less-expressive people can come across as uninterested in the conversation or as not being a thinking contributor. Whether that's correct or not, hundreds of expressive people in my audiences have used those very descriptions. For the more-expressive folks, they can be seen as having a nervous, frenetic energy that doesn't know when to quit. They can seem uninterested in what others have to say and may seem uncomfortable with silence. Again, this is taken from hundreds of less-expressive participants in workshops describing their opposites. So, it's an even playing field, and the world is lovelier because we have all sorts of noise levels, from silence to cacophony, to keep us interested.

ACTIVATION

- Most of us in our careers have been measured on our baseline expressiveness. But if you haven't, rank yourself according to the following unscientific scale:

  ◦ When you walk into a room full of people who you don't know, if you are likely to jump in and introduce yourself and mingle freely, openly sharing things about yourself without being prompted, you are in the expressiveness range of 6-7.

  ◦ If you walk into the room and look around for friendly faces, find smaller groups of people, and are willing to share, but are more likely to ask about others and wait to be asked about yourself, rank yourself in the 3-5 range.

  ◦ And, if you're most likely to walk into that room full of strangers and feel anxiety or let people come to you and wait for others to ask about you or are more comfortable when you say "Tell me about yourself" and hope they chat the night away, you can rank yourself in the 1-2 range.

Ego Strength

Expression levels are important, but they aren't the whole story. They just help others experience the behaviors that accompany what we believe about ourselves: ego strength.

Some of the most profound lessons we can learn about business and life come from the seemingly mundane events. One of the most important for me—a lesson about ego strength, and about being a decent human being—came to me all because of an idiotic wrestling match.

I come from a large family, five boys and two girls. We wrestled growing up because my father was a champion wrestler in his youth. Me, my sisters, my mom—everybody wrestled. I was the youngest son for a long time, and I always lost. It was always me on the bottom of a wrestling dogpile and, frankly, I got sick of losing. And then one day when I was six years old, my mom brought a child into this world. For me. My little brother, Terry. The moment he came home, I could roll his helpless little body over and pin him whenever I wanted. It was the tacit rule. I was six years older, six years bigger; sometimes he would just look at me, lie down, and pin himself.

Decades later, Terry decided to marry. He was thirty-two, and at that point in his life, he and his fiancée, Jacki, were firmly entrenched in the Boulder, Colorado, lifestyle. Bark and granola for breakfast, meadow flowers and soy milk, no shaving for anyone—they were the quintessential earth muffins. Terry asked if he could have his wedding reception in my backyard because I have a nice garden; that would happen after his streamside wedding, complete with fishing poles and a wedding dress worn with hiking boots.

That hot August afternoon when he had his reception, some 125 earthy Boulder pacifists adorned my backyard, noshing on tofu burritos and strawberry margaritas laced with vitamin C crystals. After having downed a few of those, things got interesting.

Terry and I put our drinks down and before we knew it, we were wrestling in the middle of the backyard. It was all fun and games at first, but Terry had forgotten the tacit rule from growing up: I was supposed to win. He wasn't going down. Soon, the gaggle of pacifists encircled us, confused by this display of brotherly love.

With an audience, we turned up the heat on the performance. I went to grab for Terry's head, but my watchband grabbed the tiniest little piece of neck flesh instead. Do you know how bloody a little nick on the neck can get? It was everywhere. The pacifists were now hollering like Romans watching gladiators. My mom and Jacki were crying for us to stop.

At this point I thought, "Too bad if it's your wedding. My house, my rules—you're going down." So I rushed at Terry, picked him up, threw him down, and pinned him immediately. On the way down, I tore muscles in my leg and lower back. Terry decided to put his eyeball on my elbow. The white of his eye became the red of his eye. Quite messy, and it looked a lot worse than it actually was. These things heal quickly, you know.

We ended our match looking like two goobers, all bloody and smiling like idiots. We were hurt, but I won. People talked about the wrestling match for a long, long time. It taught me about life and is something I teach in workshops today.

Here's the lesson to take from my backyard wrestling match.

When I wrestled Terry on that steamy August day, I was thirty-eight years old. I was no longer in my lithe and more muscular fifteen-year-old body. And so, to win I had to hurt both him and me. I was no longer *strong enough to be gentle*. The strong ego is like that—it is a gentle one. It doesn't have to hurt you in order to make its point. It doesn't have to be right every step of the way, and it looks for win/win situations. The strong ego fully realizes that we're all unfinished human beings and that *together* we might actually get something done.

The weak ego, on the other hand, is fragile and supremely unconfident. It's a bully. It's all right for it to get hurt, just so long as the other person gets hurt more. The weak ego needs to be right at all costs and will own just about every good idea that comes along, because of course, they already had the idea before you or me. The weak ego is brilliant at deflecting blame. It's defensive. It's not self-aware, so it doesn't notice that every time there's a problem, it happens to be present.

"Strong enough to be gentle" is the point I want to draw here. Had I been in a strong ego state that day, I would not have needed to win at all costs. It was the man's wedding after all—he should have won, no matter what.

I'd venture to say that all of us have some of the weak and some of the strong sides of the ego floating around in our repertoire. Successful people work daily to keep their ego strong, and on some days, with some people, it takes a good deal of effort to keep it that way. But they do it anyway.

Here is the ego chart again. Let's take a brief look at each of the quadrants to help you determine when you're in each—and so you can make more deliberate choices to get where you want to be. Suffice it to say, the strong-ego side of the chart is linked to positive and attractive behaviors, while the weak side is negative and repellant. Again, we're all going to have a combination of those throughout our lives. The goal is to recognize when we are on the weak side or when we're causing others to be on the weak side so that we can choose to do something about it.

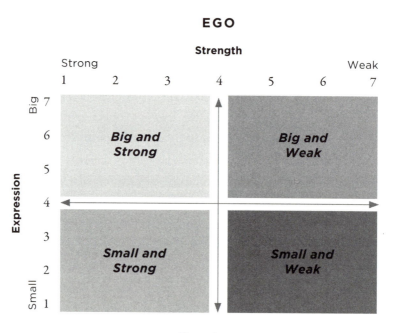

EGO

Figure 2

THE SMALL, WEAK EGO

The small (less expressive), weak ego is something of a mixed bag, falling into two categories that play out a little bit differently: the unworthy and the victim. People who fall in this quadrant tend to be lacking in confidence, timid, shy, or passive-aggressive. They might see their introversion as a liability as opposed to a positive attribute.

As victims, their attitude is resentful and filled with contempt, which others might have a difficult time understanding due to these people's lack of expression. They usually won't speak up in a meeting—that's not what they do. But when they leave the meeting, they might find a trusted confidante and sabotage the meeting afterward, tearing apart everything they agreed to by not voicing their dissent earlier.

The unworthy part of the small, weak ego is more timid and feels—well, unworthy. People like this believe that all of the good things happen to other people. They can have a very passive attitude and are difficult to read because of their lack of expression. They don't believe they are worthy of attention from others, and they don't seek it out. Many describe this ego affect as pathetic.

Here are some of the attributes of people in this quadrant. They are . . .

- Unconfident.
- "Me-centric"—focused on their own needs or their own world.
- Emotional vampires. Without knowing it, they require a lot of our energy for us to be around them. We are always checking in, wondering if there is something wrong or telling them that indeed they are doing a fine job.
- Needy.
- Quiet.
- Pessimistic.
- Lonely.
- Socially awkward or do not desire social interaction.
- **People who embody this ego quadrant:** George Costanza from *Seinfeld*, serial killer Jeffrey Dahmer (lots of other things going on there, but his profile fits in this box), Eeyore from Winnie-the-Pooh, and all of us when we're sick or have received devastating news.

The difficult thing about this quadrant is that when we're in it, we need some help to get out. Often, though, we don't feel worthy, or we feel we don't need others' help, so we don't seek it out or accept it when it's offered. Here's the message: When you are in a vulnerable situation—sick, fired, demoted, demoralized—surrender to the help you are offered.

A quick note on what to do about people you might find yourself entangled with who are in this quadrant at work or home. This is a tough box to manage anyone out of. Most of us are not equipped as professional psychologists to help people from this box; it's a career in and of itself. You can be there for people, though. Also recognize that when we find ourselves entering into the small, weak ego space, it is sometimes a natural reaction to bad news or events.

My sister Meg was doing a home move a long time ago. It was one of those more-awful-than-usual moves; she had a lot of emotional ties to the place she was leaving and very few connections—other than more pay and more job responsibility—to the place she was going. She really wanted to stay in her old place, but alas, a far better job in a worse place presented itself. We were talking on the phone one day, and she was heavily lamenting this move. Mistaking her sullen mood as a cry for help, I offered her a pep talk, along with advice and insights about why I thought this was such a great move (it's not always a good thing to have a personal/professional-development speaker as a brother). She quickly said, "Scott, there's nothing to solve here. I don't need your advice. I just need you to listen. I need to feel bad about this for a little bit; will you just let me do that?" Wiser words have rarely been spoken. It's important to tread carefully with people in this space (including yourself), because sometimes they just need to vent, or be in a quiet place and work through it themselves.

On the other hand, we may need to be a little more forceful when someone believes they don't need any assistance, but clearly do. Our dear friend and colleague who is as strong as they come (we'll call her Janice) found herself in this quadrant when she was going through a separation from a man (let's call him Brad) she dearly loved but couldn't live with anymore. His addiction to dangerous, adrenaline-filled activities was not conducive to a marriage and two small children. During their separation, Brad was in a horrible accident. He broke his back and ended up in a coma. That's bad, bad news by anyone's standards, and Janice went into protection mode. She took care of her comatose husband, her two children, her parents, Brad's parents—but not herself. She got more and more haggard-looking as time went on and began to lose an alarming amount of weight. She became introspective and isolated herself in a world that was about only managing others. She was needy but didn't know it.

My business partner, Marty, decided to take things into her own hands. She called Janice and told her she was stealing her away for a spa weekend. Janice put up all kinds of barriers to that offer of help, listing for Marty all the many reasons she absolutely could not leave: Brad, kids, business, parents. The list was exhaustive. Marty told her, "Your mom is here to babysit the kids, Brad is in a coma in the hospital in stable condition, and you are coming with me."

They went. I don't know what women do on "girls' weekends," but something miraculous must take place. Janice came back ready to face this huge trial in her life. At this writing, Brad is mostly healed and is still busy trying to conquer the next frontier, but more measuredly now, and Janice is back to her amazing, confident, and strong self.

Sometimes, when we are proactive—when we notice something is off with a colleague with an otherwise strong ego—it's just the right thing to be a little more assertive. The small, weak ego is prone to missing its own misery.

ACTIVATION

- Do you know anyone in this box who needs an assertive intervention?

- When have you been in this box?

- Are you willing to surrender when you're sick or going through some sort of trauma?

- Who in your life will you always trust, even if you don't want to hear their honest appraisal?

THE BIG, WEAK EGO

The big (more expressive), weak ego is hands-down most people's favorite quadrant to hate on. When I move over into this box myself, it always feels bad, and I'm always left regretting my actions and/or words. A lot of the more insensitive ladder-climbers in the world can be found in this box most of the time.

As we discuss the big, weak ego, think about times when you've been in this quadrant. We're a lot better at seeing when others are in it, but it's important to know when we have stepped over the line into this space. When this ego walks into the room, we might sense a little negative shift because they command attention—only it's the bad kind. These people are . . .

- Charming—until we disagree with them.
- Abrasive.
- Bold.
- Manipulative—sometimes in a charming way.
- Aggressive and passive-aggressive.
- Unconfident (though you might not guess it because of their show of bravado)—they're afraid we might discover they aren't everything they want us to believe they are.
- Bullies.
- Constantly in need of being right, at all costs. Avoid directly pointing out their flaws or times when they are wrong, especially in front of a group of people. If you do, they will hunt you down and exact vengeance—maybe not now, but definitely sometime down the road. You've probably had bosses who fit this description.
- Defensive.
- Diminishing of others, rather than enlarging.
- Arrogant.
- Gossips and saboteurs.
- And many other negative adjectives you can think of that probably fit in this box.
- **People who embody this ego quadrant:** Jack Nicholson in *A Few Good Men* ("You can't handle the truth!"), Idi Amin, bosses who regularly do not give credit where it is due.

If you want clues on how to deal with a big, weak ego, go back to the section on David Rock's SCARF model (chapter 3) and remind yourself of all of those threats, because this type of ego ultimately becomes negatively sensitive to all of them. Those in this ego quadrant are sensitive to a lot of things, because their sense of themselves is frail underneath all that bluster. They are scanning the environment for slights and threats to their status, and they're also searching—even more so—for approval.

When we are in agreement with the big, weak ego, we don't have to pay as much attention to our communication style as when we disagree with them. The knee-jerk reaction when we do disagree with a big, weak ego is usually to let them have a piece of our mind. They often bring out the weak side of our own ego, and a personality collision ensues. Neuroscience labs have even studied why we like to get back at someone with a big, weak ego. The answer is *Schadenfreude*, a German word for the pleasure we derive from someone else's misfortune; we want to prove them wrong so we can enjoy the fallout. This shows up as a reward in the brain,[1] so there is a strong pull toward wanting to experience it. It's like the time a maniac driver was riding my bumper, and then pulled out from behind me, stepped on the gas pedal, gave me the middle finger, and sped forward—and was pulled over by cops moments later. I thought about going around the block just to gloat (I wanted more of that intoxicating *Schadenfreude*), but then my prefrontal cortex took over and I kept going.

Avoid succumbing to the allure of this "gotcha" feeling when dealing with a big, weak ego. Instead, choose to slow down and think about what you're going to say. Do not get pulled into the trap of back-and-forth defending. For the most part, nothing good ever comes of that. My policy is *when in doubt, ask questions*. That's my main strategy for keeping my own ego out of the big, weak quadrant in a conversation that pushes my buttons. It's important to make sure the questions we ask aren't based in resentment, such as "Okay, so if you know everything, what would you do?" Instead, ask sincere questions—those to which you really don't know the answer.

In the section on collaboration that's coming up, I present a formula that works for all of us who want to explore and collaborate, and it works with big, weak egos too.

THE BIG, STRONG EGO AND THE SMALL, STRONG EGO

When we're on the strong side of the chart or are in the presence of someone who is, it feels good, even great. I've noticed that when I'm in the presence of strong egos, I like myself better. It's become an acid test for me: Do I make people feel good about themselves for having been in my presence? The entire strong side is about enlarging others. Strong egos are interested—truly interested—in things and people beyond themselves. The use of active-constructive responding puts us on the strong side of the ego chart.

The strong ego's mantra is "I am no longer interested in being right; I am only interested in what works." The strong ego is able to more appropriately express its thoughts, desires, and emotions so the person moves up and down the expression side of the chart more fluidly. The more expressive strong egos know when it makes sense to shrink, and the less expressive strong egos know when it's appropriate to speak up. The strong ego is easier to be with, because we don't have to prepare for the encounter as we do with the weak ego. We can typically be more ourselves; there seems to be an unwritten understanding that we are all just unfinished human beings on a journey together. To a strong ego, a half-baked idea is just an invitation to get it fully cooked through *interactive flow*, something you'll understand to be a powerful tool once we discuss it in the next chapter.

Harvard University anthropologist and psychoanalyst Michael Maccoby writes in his book *The Productive Narcissist* that excellent leaders are productive narcissists. They believe they can change their companies, if not the world. But there's a big difference between them and the unproductive narcissist. The productive narcissist believes they need our help. The unproductive narcissist— those with weak egos, especially big, weak egos—may believe they can change the world but don't need or want our help.

Here are some other attributes that define the big (more expressive), strong ego:

- Confident
- Gregarious
- Opinionated
- Optimistic
- Generous
- Great teachers

- Encouraging
- Willing to change their mind in the face of new information
- Charismatic
- Lives with a purpose and values
- **People who embody this ego quadrant:** Oprah Winfrey, Jeffrey Immelt, Richard Branson, Seth Godin, Colin Powell.

And here are some attributes of the small (less expressive), strong ego:

- Confident
- Active listeners
- Engaged
- Great mentors
- Lead by example
- Share the spotlight
- Humble
- Values-driven
- Optimistic
- **People who embody this ego quadrant:** Martin Luther King Jr., Gandhi, Mother Teresa, Warren Buffett.

You get to choose which side of the chart you're on. I don't have to launch into a diatribe here for you to see which side makes the most sense in every way. People sometimes ask me if there's ever a good reason to be on the weak side of the chart. I tell them, "Only when you're having a bad day, but don't forget to ask forgiveness from all those around you when you've popped over the line." And indeed, we will all pop over the line at times. With this new awareness, you can now decide if that's where you want to be.

The trick to being and staying on the strong side of the chart is possessing a combination of attributes. An open attitude toward the contribution of others laced with a realistic appraisal of our own abilities, along with the confidence we discussed earlier, are three key factors. These attributes combine to allow us to create significance with, through, and for others. The strong ego's nature is to assume the best of others while accurately understanding that the great, successful people of the world did it alongside others. It's a mindset that takes practice, especially when we're met with challenging weak egos who might easily pull us over onto their side of the line. When we feel criticized, we are more vulnerable to the weak ego and risk hopping over the line to join it. Be aware of the circumstances that have a tendency to bring about your weak-ego self and avoid them when you can. For instance, if you know that a certain person always pushes your buttons and you're feeling particularly susceptible, save your interaction with that individual for a time when you're feeling more confident and generous. If you can't avoid the conflict, stay strong by listening more than you speak. Practice ACR. Take a little more time to respond so that your interaction doesn't become only about refuting each other's points of view. That kind of communication can escalate into both of you becoming weak. Of course, it's an entirely different kind of disagreement if you and the other person are both on the strong side of the chart. Then it's a debate of an idea to make it better, not a tearing down of the individuals involved in order to prove who is right.

ACTIVATION

- Make a copy of the ego chart on a piece of paper.

- Write down the initials of the five to ten people you work with the most on a daily or weekly basis.

- According to your experience with them, place them on the chart according to where you feel they are most of the time when you're working with them. Mine looks like this:

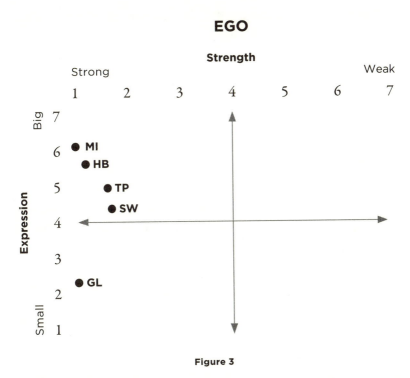

Figure 3

You'll notice that all my dots are on the positive side of the chart. That's an amazing situation to be in. Marty and I own our company, so we get to choose the people we work with the most. You might not be as fortunate, and you may have inherited some individuals who struggle with ego weakness. Look back at your chart. The more dots you have on the weak side, the more exhausted you probably are at the end of the day, because you're busy doing adult daycare. Much of your time is likely spent on managing negative emotions and sensitive people rather than getting to the real issues at hand or being innovative and creative. For those of you with all of your dots charted on the strong side, work very hard to keep that. It's a gift.

Ask yourself the following questions:

- When I judge someone to be on the weak side of the chart, is that how they generally are in most people's eyes, or do I cause them to go weak when I'm around them? (Be careful not to discern this by creating a gossip campaign about the other person just to prove that you're right. That's a weak-ego trick. Instead, simply observe the individual's interactions with others when you can.)

- Where would I place my dot on the ego chart?
- Where would others place my dot?
- Where would the weak egos in my life place my dot?
- Where would the weak egos in my life place their dot?
- What am I going to do to change that relationship?

When we understand our part in the social interactions we have, we can begin to choose the kind of impact we have on others more frequently. Your ego is part of you, and the healthier and stronger you keep it, the more effective you'll be as a member of teams that are cooperating and collaborating to achieve a common goal.

Egos are a fact of being human and alive—there's no such thing as getting the ego out of a room. It will always be there. Rather than trying to get rid of it, we want to pay attention to its strength. Understanding and being aware of your ego strength can make work more enjoyable. Plus, strong-ego teams operate on a higher plane and are better able to think together and actually disagree with each other. That lets us use one of the most powerful tools of the human brain and an important one for individuals and organizations that want to grow and prosper: collaboration, the subject of the next chapter.

CHAPTER 15

Collaboration: The Ultimate Survival Tool of Humans

YOU WOULD NOT BE READING this right now if our ancestors hadn't worked together. The dangerous world they lived in required them to rally together to find ways to survive. There was hunting and foraging, tending children and the fire, guarding the homestead, protecting each other from the outside world—and all of it had to be done by small clans. Being the relatively physically weak species we are, we would have died off in short order had we acted alone. Collaborating is literally ages old, and still we need to be reminded about why and how to work together to create better lives.

The first thing to keep in mind, and probably one of the most compelling arguments for working together, is that we're smarter together. The evidence keeps piling up. James Surowiecki's *The Wisdom of Crowds* discusses many pieces of evidence that point to the notion that no one genius on a topic is smarter than an average group of people on the same topic. We are better together in so many ways, and yet we are often tempted to set out on our own so *we* get the prize and acknowledgment. Those can still be ours when we collaborate, though—and we have a better product or idea at the end of the day.

Working well with others makes us smarter and better at what we do. On a recent episode of *The Voice* (yes, I'm a groupie), Grammy Award–winning singer Miranda Lambert was coaching two contestants during a rehearsal for their competition in the show's Battle Round. They would be singing a duet together, and at the end of that performance, their judge would decide which one to keep. This particular duo was competing against each other very rigorously, singing over each other during rehearsals. Finally Miranda stopped them in frustration and said, "You're two different singers singing your own great version of the song. If you don't make it look like a performance together, you'll both end up looking bad." We can all benefit from her advice, including in situations at work. How often do we compete against each other, when all the evidence shows that working together benefits us so much more? When you find yourself competing, check in frequently to make sure that you're meshing—that you're still singing the same song. If you don't, you stand a greater chance of putting out an inferior work product. Working together produces the opposite result.

Collaboration has the added bonus of making us feel more joy than when we go it alone. Recall from our discussion of the powerful bonding hormone oxytocin that collaboration is one of the things we can do to bring about trust (via a release of oxytocin). Collaboration can be a productive and euphoric state if we can manage our egos and actually work together. As radical as this may sound, that means that work can be a source of sheer joy. When we're working well with others toward a common goal, we achieve greater feelings of significance and satisfaction.

WORKING AS PART OF A TEAM BRINGS US JOY AND MAKES US SMARTER

Psychologist Mihaly Csikszentmihalyi, a researcher of optimal human experience, defined his concept of flow in his book *Flow: The Psychology of Optimal Experience*. Flow is the euphoric state one falls into when performing a skill they have practiced. The person in flow loses track of time; the activity feels easy to perform; there is a lack of self-consciousness—the ego is in check. That is flow. And the research is showing that flowing together with others is even more powerful than being in flow alone.

Psychologist Charles Walker takes the idea of individual flow and broadens it to two other states: coactive flow and interactive flow.[1] *Coactive flow* is when we work in the presence of others, like a group of financial analysts working on their own projects in the same room with others and sharing information back and forth. Walker found that when test subjects did something like this, they reported more joy and productivity than when doing it entirely alone. Then Walker wanted to investigate further. He found that the highest sense of euphoria and effectiveness were reported during *interactive flow*. This is when we work together and share our talents toward a common goal. Walker began testing his hypothesis with volleyball players. The teams that were instructed to be coactive—hitting the ball over the net without the help of others—described less joy and effectiveness than those that were instructed to be interactive, who were told that the ball had to be hit by at least two people before it was hit over the net.

Think about how this might apply to work teams. Is your team a group of people all working together but separately? Or are you actually "passing the ball" before giving the big proposal to a client? Think about asking colleagues, "Would you look at my proposal and tell me what you think is missing?" Discussion, debate, and input will make the proposal better. And yet we often go it alone. This could be in part a cultural issue. In the Western world, individualism is rewarded. In Eastern cultures, however, working together is the norm. Companies in the United States have been trying for decades to bring the Eastern style of teamwork to the workplace. Centuries of culture are difficult to change, but adapting to the idea of interactive flow could be a start.

Even though it makes us feel important to be the one with *the* idea, science is showing us that we really are better together—that, as Tom Cruise said as Jerry Maguire in the 1996 movie of the same name, "you complete me." There are great examples of this in nature. Consider Eric Fortune's recent work on plain-tailed wrens—yes, birds.[2] He illustrates how male and female wrens chirp in an alternating duet so rapidly that it sounds as if one bird is singing. They cooperate to produce one song. Can humans do the same? Fortune contends that human cooperation instincts are not too different. Our greatest impact at work and in the world will likely be with others, and completing something together gives us an enormous dopamine bump—and an intense feeling of well-being.

If you don't find experiencing joy at work a persuasive argument for collaborating, consider the fact that collaboration can also make you smarter. A study coauthored by researchers at MIT, Carnegie Mellon University, and Union College found that working together can increase the overall intelligence of a team.[3] There is much to the study, but here are the three attributes the researchers consistently found predicted higher collective intelligence in teams:

- The even distribution of turn-taking in the team
- The degree of social sensitivity in the group (knowing each other outside the topic and using empathy)
- The distribution of women to men: 60 percent women and 40 percent men (at baseline, women are generally better at the first two points of a collectively intelligent team)

Nearly seven hundred test subjects proved over and over again that the overall performance of the group had little to do with the individual capabilities of those in the group. They found that the pooling of experience and skill elevated the entire group.

All is not lost for teams that are very unbalanced in gender. While the research shows that females are generally better at social sensitivity and are largely more collaborative (turn-taking) than men, who are often more competitive, the good news is that turn-taking and social sensitivity can be taught.

At your next meeting, consider sharing these powerful findings and reset the rules of engagement during meetings. Make it easy for everyone in the meeting to share (a good team size is five to seven people). See if you get better results. Pay attention to the mood of the group when everyone gets to participate.

ACTIVATION

- Create an in-house site where your team can upload work they would like others to add their insights to.

- Create a new ground rule for yourself and/or your team: No important product, project, or proposal goes out the door without at least three other people adding their expertise and insights.

- Share with your team the research on how turn-taking and collaboration increase group intelligence. Let those attributes characterize all your meetings.

START BY GETTING TO KNOW YOUR TEAM AND HOW YOU ALL CONTRIBUTE

There are teams that will naturally slip into interactively working together, but there are probably more that need to be coached and convinced that this "passing the ball" style of working is better and more efficient. When everyone understands how they fit into the grand scheme of things—that without them the team will not operate as well—engagement will likely be easier to facilitate. Interestingly, one of the greatest teachers of this lesson is the common pencil.

No single person on the planet knows how to create something as simple as a pencil. Leonard Read made that seemingly exaggerated assertion more than fifty years ago in his famous essay *I, Pencil*. No one could make a pencil on their own: not the president of the company, not the pencil salespeople, not the manufacturers of the pencil. No single human knows how to do everything required to make a pencil. Mr. Read opines on the hundreds of operations that go into it, from chainsaws used to chop down the mighty cedars; to the castor beans needed to create the lacquer on the pencil; to the oil industry, which is needed to manufacture the pencil shaft; to the mining of the graphite that goes inside. And, that's just a pencil. Extrapolate Read's thinking to the complex products and services offered by your company, and the case for internal cooperation is evident.

One of the most important factors in building safety and trust within a team—and thus upping the team's collective intelligence and critical-thinking ability—is how well group members know each other outside their work together. Getting this added context on colleagues is a powerful learning tool for the brain.

In critical-thinking meetings, set up a context-setting meeting as a first step. If a group is set to debate and solve issues around a major software issue, for instance, the context-setting meeting could unfold like this. The first step would be to have the members spend time getting to know each other. This can be tackled in a variety of ways. One group asked team members to bring a favorite picture of themselves doing a hobby or on vacation—anything that would shine light on them outside their work. They each got five minutes to talk about their picture and its background. It might sound a little trite, but the research suggests that it's one of the smartest things we can do to be smarter as a group.

The second step of the meeting might be to give context on the topic at hand. Everyone in the meeting could talk about their experience with the topic and the strength they believe they bring to the team. One client began her meeting by handing out T-shirts with blank shields on them. She gave her team colored markers and told them to design their shield based on the superhero strength they bring to the team. Each team member got to present their T-shirt and strength. The result was fun, insightful, nonthreatening, and a great way for people to brag a bit. It also illustrated how each of them was needed to round out the strength of the team.

The combination of common purpose, stamina, and collective intelligence is an excellent equation for collaborating to create significance and an impact in your organization.

ACTIVATION

- Flow is good. Coactive flow is better. And when it comes to group effectiveness, interactive flow is best. Work with your team to learn how to "pass the ball."

- Work on collaborating instead of competing. When you get stuck, ask colleagues, "What am I missing?" Listen to the answer.

- Have your team read *I, Pencil* and then discuss the ideas behind it, including the importance of collaboration.

- Ask team members to describe what piece of the pencil they bring to your organization and to the team. This is a particularly helpful exercise at the beginning of a project.

COMMUNICATE TO COLLABORATE

Part of the point of collaborating is finding out how we can take an idea and make it work. Recall our discussion about the ego—the strong ego is interested in what works, not in being right or getting its own ideas validated. That means strong egos are great for collaborating. The following model, intended to help you collaborate through communication, will even work for those pesky weak egos, however.

Explore for Agreement

The first step is a thought-finding mission. We don't have to agree with everything, but if we want to get the conversation rolling in a positive, collaborative direction, we have to find some place of agreement. In negotiation circles, it's well understood that the person with the most information has the upper hand. You already know what you believe and why. This is your opportunity not to share those thoughts quite yet, but to explore the other person's thinking. Ask questions about how others are viewing an issue. You want to get their viewpoint. Again, this can't be stressed enough, ask questions out of curiosity, not testing. Testing questions sound like "Did you try this or that?" Of course they did if they are a big, weak ego. That kind of testing could be the death knell of rapport with them. Remember, they will likely tell you that they have tried everything you can think of. Don't interrogate or use the Socratic method, whereby you ask them questions that eventually lead them to see the error in their thinking and the wisdom in yours. The smart ones will see this coming; plus, it feels like a legal deposition. Try question/statements: "Tell me your thinking on this." Ask questions based on their answer. Offer an idea and ask the other person what you're missing. That's one of my favorites, because it says you're open for feedback and it opens the door for the other person to interact with the idea. If your discussion is about something you disagree on, exploring helps bring you together. Eventually, you will most likely discover some point of agreement. That's where you want to exclaim that you can now see where they are coming from. Now you are in forward motion as opposed to the standstill or backward motion of defending back and forth.

Detach from Being Right

It's easy to believe our idea is the *one* solution everyone's been looking for. You may be correct that your idea is better. But it rarely works to throw it out there and say, "See, this is what's really right!" Detach yourself from the need to prove you're right. Adopt the mindset that your idea is one of many other ideas in the room, even though some ideas are the polar opposite of yours. Somewhere in each idea could lie a kernel of truth that can be incorporated into the solution. Remember, collaboration is about finding the one *idea* that works, not the one *person* who's right.

Add or Modify

If indeed you want to explore your ideas after you have come to a place of understanding, present the idea by asking questions like "What do you think of . . . ?" and "How would this go with your idea about . . . ?" This approach—adding your own idea rather than negating the other person's—is a safe way to add ideas on to the position of a big, weak ego. See where the conversation goes as you explore adding to the idea. It is actually fun when you get out of the weak place of needing to be right and instead move to the strong position of exploring what works.

One point of caution: Big, weak egos might have a tendency to make the newly formed idea their own. That comes with the territory. It's an unpleasant fact of dealing with this ego type. If you really need others to know that you are a part of the newly formed idea, make sure you communicate it to others first; that you include both your and the big, weak ego's name on it; and that you detail the efforts both of you made to come to this solution.

This simple approach to collaborating on an idea can result in testy moments, and that's fine. Opposing viewpoints and dissonance create disruption in status-quo thinking and interrupt groupthink—the kind of thinking that happens when a team is tired and just rubberstamps an idea so everyone can move on. A lot of average thinking happens in groups that don't feel safe enough to disagree. However, when a team keeps its focus on the issue and not the person who is representing the idea, big things can happen.

ACTIVATION

- Explore another's ideas, especially if you disagree. Find out where you might agree on some aspect of their thinking.

- Detach from needing to be right and from trying to convince others how right you are. Remember, it's not a competition for rightness, but rather a collaboration to find what works.

- Add to or modify ideas that you disagree with. Use "Yes, and . . ." to open your rebuttal, not "But . . ." This will give the conversation a sense of safety and collaboration.

Collaboration is nothing new, but the science about what we get from it keeps emerging, illustrating to us that we don't have to do our work alone, that we actually shouldn't be the lone wolf we often find ourselves being. The old adage "If you want something done right, do it yourself" should more accurately read "If you want something done the way *you want it done*, do it yourself." Plus, people who work interactively and collaboratively have more fun and create a better work product.

Your impact on the world doesn't have to be about inventing new technology or making groundbreaking discoveries. The significance you create doesn't have to come with a big title, and more often than not it doesn't. Your impact and the significance you create have to do with deciding to collaborate well—the way humans have for millennia.

As Robert Fulghum so profoundly put it in his famous book *All I Really Need to Know I Learned in Kindergarten*:

> Think what a better world it would be if we all—the whole world—had cookies and milk about three o'clock every afternoon and then lay down with our blankies for a nap. Or if all governments had as a basic policy to always put things back where they found them and to clean up their own mess.
>
> And it is still true, no matter how old you are—when you go out into the world, it is best to hold hands and stick together.

Choose Now

===

THERE IS NO WAY WE can know the entire capability of the human brain. It will be a long time before we get there, if we ever do. Scientists often want to wait until every *i* is dotted and each *t* is crossed before they release anything definitive. That's the nature of science. The information we have now, however, gives us enough to make some pretty good guesses. Plus, we have those guts and senses and life experience that often tell us what's truly right; it's not always necessary to have an enormous longitudinal, double-blind, randomized, controlled study with factor analyses and *p*-values and *t*-tests and regression analyses and so on—all of this usually ends up confirming what our guts are already telling us. Science gives it the teeth, certainly, but science can also get into hair-splitting that our nuanced brains don't really need in order to understand what makes intuitive sense. Neuroscientists, psychologists, sociologists, and anthropologists are collectively working on understanding the human brain and how it compels our species forward, but we don't have to wait until they arrive at the answer to start reaping the benefits of what we know now.

As we sit with ourselves each day and explore the big questions of life and existence, we can work on answering those gaping questions by creating the answers for ourselves. We get to decide what kind of significance we want to create and learn how to use the brain to get there. We can do that better when we understand our biology, particularly that of the brain. Even if we only have a low-level understanding of how it all works, it gives us the control we need to make a difference. If we spend our time in ignorance, constantly running from stress and perceived threats, our energy will be spent simply trying to survive.

But we can put the brain in a safer, more controlled place, one that allows us to create, interact, and even disagree productively. When we know what we can control and pay attention to what brings out the best in us, we get more of that. From there, we're released from the toxicity of focusing on the negative aspects of the world, and we become profoundly more positively energized—and energizing to those around us. That's when stamina kicks in; we have to be able to keep it up.

Stamina is ours when we choose the right inputs for the holes in our heads. Ask yourself every day what's going into your ears, eyes, mouth, and nose. We don't always get a say, but we have more say than we might think. Bask in things that make you feel alive and connected. Every company I know wants smart, alive, open-minded, and connected employees. Executives might not use those words to describe the attributes of successful employees, but these words do describe how they talk about the perfect colleague. The energy you create in yourself is felt several times over from those around you. Try some of the things we talked about and see if you begin to get different positive responses in your life. I would love to hear about those experiences.

And finally there is significance. There are those who will always believe that their world only gets better when the circumstances of the world align in their favor. But you now understand how to align your world in a way that paves the way for finding and creating significance; you get to create and direct the conversations that lead to real change in your world. It's a choice that begins with awareness and continues with taking the steps we outlined for creating significance.

Organizational psychologist Manfred F. R. Kets de Vries was asked once if there was ever a time when we could know too much about ourselves, when we could become too self-aware. He answered with an analogy, something like this: If we knew all there was to know about ourselves, it would be like owning a magnificent mansion, walking in at evening time, and being met with fluorescent lights illuminating every corner of the home. Not only would it be difficult to look at—and sometimes ugly—but it would also be uninteresting. There wouldn't be any mystery or shadows to bring intrigue. The human brain might be like that; perhaps it's best to shed enough light on it to see our way around, but not so much that we lose the mystery that makes us interesting. Sometimes knowing and sensing the world by Braille—by feeling it in the dark—tells us much more than all of the floodlights in the world could reveal about human behavior.

At the end of the day, all the studies and books written about the brain, all of the machinery that lets us look at biological processes as they are happening, all of the blood tests that tell us about genetic markers of who we might be—all of those things, in my opinion, will never replace what we think and experience and the choices we make because of what our intuition tells us. Sometimes finding our way means getting lost and finding our way all over again. During that journey, we learn about the unique star that we represent in human history. During the quest to know, we find out that maybe we never can know—so we get to make new and interesting choices for the rest of our time here on this planet.

What you do next is up to you. Just remember one thing: Start small, start now. Activate.

Acknowledgments

THIS BRAINCHILD IS THE product of the collective neurons of so many people; each one I feel connected to in a very deep and meaningful way. There are far more people to thank than we have pages for, but I would like to acknowledge those who made a true impact on the genesis of this book. As a species, our ability to express our deepest gratitude is probably best suited to an in-person, look-in-my-eyeballs kind of encounter. Barring that luxury, I have to resort to words to try to do the thank you justice; and here I will try.

If there ever was a miracle worker, it is my editor, Lari Bishop. You are brilliant beyond compare, compassionate at just the right moment, and as beautifully honest as anyone I have ever met. I could have written an entire chapter about the marvels of your wisdom and your wit. But then you would have edited it out. Thank you for being such a caring shepherd. Without you . . . well, you saw the first draft. This book would not be a book.

Aaron Hierholzer, you are a gift. Your firm, thoughtful hand in editing is one of the best examples of how humans make each other smarter. Your brain power is evident throughout this book.

Peter Mende-Siedlecki, you are one of the universe's brightest stars, and I am so grateful I get to bask in your light. Your brilliance in neuroscience and psychology and your ability to help translate those complex findings into useable ideas is astonishing. Thank you for keeping me on track.

Early in my work in the neuroscience of success, a client and now a true friend, Kimberly Kleiman-Lee, pushed and prodded me to take what I teach in the corporation and put it into the words you see in this book. A few gray hairs later, here it is. *Mwah!*

It all began several years ago at the NeuroLeadership Summit put on by David Rock and Alan Ringleb. Through the NeuroLeadership Institute I was able to deepen my learning about the mysteries of the brain and make connections with some of the brightest brains in the brain world. Thank you both for your inspiration and for creating an entirely new "neural pathway" to thinking about leadership. My brain was stretched and challenged as I schooled it in the intricacies and nuances of what we know about the brain by the genius of my professors Drs. Golnaz Tabibnia and Josh Davis.

One of the most important elements of writing is to walk away, rewrite, and then have people smarter than you look at it and make their contribution. Thank you to my fellow colleagues of the NeuroPractitioners' Guild—Linda Hayes, Carla Street, Tiffany Gray. Each of you will find your thoughts and touches in the pages here.

Clint Greenleaf, the namesake of my publisher, got on the bandwagon for this book years before I ever found enough energy to write it. Over the years, you patiently cajoled me into getting it out of my cortex and onto paper.

Lou Heckler, you are an ever-present inspiration in my life and the unwitting creator of the basic outline of this book. We sat there right at your kitchen table as you helped me pull apart piles of information and organize it into what has become this book.

To my colleagues at Complete Intelligence, LLC: Tami Patzer, you are a calming force in my life and one very smart individual. Your candid comments on this manuscript are here in living testament to your brilliance. Sandy Wilkerson, without your steady hand running our ship, I would sink while I'm paddling so hard.

Chelsea Humbaugh, thank you for your insights and keen eye.

And finally, the Ms. in my life. Marty Lassen, you never skip a beat in supporting me in my need to do hard things like write a book. You're always there for a variety of reasons in my life and for making sure I sound smarter on paper than I actually am. You're the dearest friend I could wish for. Marty, you never doubt me, even when I do. You never cease to believe in me even when I wonder if I'm going in the right direction. Your love and support sustain me, and I always marvel at the endlessness of your capacity for both. And my mom, Moose, you precious bundle of unbridled love, I hear your voice rooting for me with every word I write. I love you.

About the Author

SCOTT HALFORD, CSP, CPAE, is an Emmy Award–winning writer and producer, an engaging presenter, and a long-time consultant to Fortune 500 executive teams. His expertise and experience enrich the contribution that he makes to every client. Scott's expansive knowledge in the areas of achievement psychology, which includes brain-based behavioral science, emotional intelligence, critical thinking, and influence, add richness and depth to his programs.

Scott's insight into the human experience at many levels, and in many different situations, allows him to communicate in workshops and keynotes with humor, wit, and depth. He is a captivating storyteller who is able to transport his audiences to destinations they may have never been physically, mentally, or emotionally. Participants laugh and learn, and consistently praise the rich and rewarding experience that positively affects their success.

Scott was inducted into the National Speakers Hall of Fame in 2014 (CPAE). He is a Certified Speaking Professional (CSP), the highest earned designation of the National Speakers Association and the Global Speakers Federation. He is also an accredited and certified Emotional Intelligence Provider as well as a Certified Associate in Emergenetics, the study of performance and preferences based on genes and the environment. Scott has an executive master's in Neuroleadership. Scott is cofounder and Principal of Complete Intelligence, LLC.

Corporate clients span many industries and include GE, Bank of America, the Walt Disney Company, Microsoft, First Data, Medtronic, Johns Hopkins

Hospital, Centura Hospitals, MillerCoors, Ingersoll-Rand, Western Union, and many more.

To book Scott for a provocative keynote or workshop, please contact Complete Intelligence at:
Email: info@completeintelligence.com
www.CompleteIntelligence.com
303-321-3953
LinkedIn, Twitter, and Facebook: Scott Halford

Notes

INTRODUCTION

1. Virginia Wise Berninger and Todd L. Richards. "The writing brain: Coordinating sensory/motor, language, and cognitive systems in working memory architecture." Pages 539–566 in V. Berninger (Ed.), *Past, Present, and Future Contributions of Cognitive Writing Research to Cognitive Psychology* (New York: Psychology Press, 2012).

THE CHOICE TO START: ACTIVATION FOR MOTIVATION

1. Barry Schwartz. *The Paradox of Choice: Why Less Is More* (New York: Ecco, 2004).

2. Nicola J. Bown, Daniel Read, and Barbara Summers. "The lure of choice." *Journal of Behavioral Decision Making* 16 (2003): 297–308.

3. Lauren A. Leotti and Mauricio R. Delgado. "The inherent reward of choice." *Psychological Science* 22 (2011): 1310–1318.

4. Martin E. P. Seligman. *Helplessness: On Depression, Development, and Death* (San Francisco: W. H. Freeman, 1975).

5. Martin E. P. Seligman. *Learned Optimism: How to Change Your Mind and Your Life* (New York: Alfred A. Knopf, 1990).

6. Frederick Herzberg. "One more time: How do you motivate employees?" *Harvard Business Review* 46 (1968): 53–62.

7. Morten L. Kringelbach and Edmund T. Rolls. "The functional neuroanatomy of the human orbitofrontal cortex: Evidence from neuroimaging and neuropsychology." *Progress in Neurobiology* 72 (2004): 341–372.

8. Samuel McClure, David I. Laibson, George Loewenstein, and Jonathan D. Cohen. "Separate neural systems value immediate and delayed monetary rewards." *Science* 306 (2004): 503–507.

9. Jessica R. Cohen and Matthew D. Lieberman. "The common neural basis of exerting self-control in multiple domains." Pages 141–162 in K. Ochsner and Y. Trope (Eds.), *From Society to Brain: The New Sciences of Self-Control* (New York: Oxford University Press).

CHAPTER 1

1. Peter Mende-Siedlecki, Christopher P. Said, and Alexander Todorov. "The social evaluation of faces: A meta-analysis of functional neuroimaging studies." *Social Cognitive and Affective Neuroscience* 8 (2013): 285–299.

2. William A. Cunningham and Tobias Brosch. "Motivational salience: Amygdala tuning from traits, needs, values, and goals." *Current Directions in Psychological Science* 21 (2012): 54–59.

3. Katerina Semendeferi, Este Armstrong, Axel Schleicher, Karl Zilles, and Gary W. Van Hoesen. "Prefrontal cortex in humans and apes: A comparative study of area 10." *American Journal of Physical Anthropology* 114 (2001): 224–241.

4. P. Thomas Schoenemann, Michael J. Sheehan, and L. Daniel Glotzer. "Prefrontal white matter volume is disproportionately larger in humans than in other primates." *Nature Neuroscience* 8 (2005): 242–252.

5. Matthew D. Lieberman. "Social cognitive neuroscience: a review of core processes." *Annual Review of Psychology* 58 (2007): 259–289.

6. David L. Van Rooy and Chockalingam Viswesvaran. "Emotional intelligence: A meta-analytic investigation of predictive validity and nomological net." *Journal of Vocational Behavior* 65 (2004): 71–95.

7. David Rosete and Joseph Ciarrochi. "Emotional intelligence and its relationship to workplace performance outcomes of leadership effectiveness." *Leadership & Organization Development Journal* 26 (2005): 388–399.

8. Elkhonon Goldberg. *The Executive Brain: Frontal Lobes and the Civilized Mind* (New York: Oxford University Press, 2001).

9. Richard L. Daft. *The Executive and the Elephant: A Leader's Guide to Building Inner Excellence.*(San Francisco: Jossey-Bass, 2010).

CHAPTER 2

1. Evian Gordon (Ed.). *Integrative Neuroscience: Bringing Together Biological, Psychological and Clinical Models of the Human Brain.* (Singapore: Harwood Academic Publishers, 2000).

2. Amy F. T. Arnsten. "The biology of being frazzled." *Science* 280 (1998): 1711–1712.

3. Karin Roelofs, Patricia Bakvis, Erno J. Hermans, Johannes van Pelt, and Jack van Honk. "The effects of social stress and cortisol responses on the preconscious selective attention to social threat." *Biological Psychology* 75 (2007): 1–7.

4. Kevin Ochsner and James J. Gross. "The cognitive control of emotion." *Trends in Cognitive Sciences* 9 (2005): 242–249.

5. Ulf Lundberg. "Stress hormones in health and illness: the roles of work and gender." *Psychoneuroendocrinology* 30 (2005): 1017–1021.

6. Wolfram Schultz. "Book review: Reward signaling by dopamine neurons." *Neuroscientist* 7 (2001): 293–302.

7. Michael Kosfeld, Markus Heinrichs, Paul J. Zak, Urs Fischbacher, and Ernst Fehr. "Oxytocin increases trust in humans." *Nature* 435 (2005): 673–676.

8. Jennifer A. Bartz, Jamil Zaki, Niall Bolger, and Kevin N. Ochsner. "Social effects of oxytocin in humans: Context and person matter." *Trends in Cognitive Sciences* 15, no. 7 (2011): 301–309.

9. Helen E. Fisher, Arthur Aron, Debra Mashek, Haifang Li, and Lucy L. Brown. "Defining the brain systems of lust, romantic attraction, and attachment." *Archives of Sexual Behavior* 31 (2002): 413–419.

CHAPTER 3

1. Kurt Lewin. "Frontiers in group dynamics." Pages 188–237 in K. Lewin, *Field Theory in Social Science: Selected Theoretical Papers*, ed. D. Cartwright (New York: Harper & Row, 1947/1951).

2. James T. Townsend and Jerome R. Busemeyer. "Approach–avoidance: Return to dynamic decision behavior." In C. Izawa (Ed.), *Current Issues in Cognitive Processes: The Tulane Flowerree Symposium on Cognition* (Hillsdale, NJ: Erlbaum, 1989): 107–133.

3. Patrik Vuilleumier. "How brains beware: Neural mechanisms of emotional attention." *Trends in Cognitive Sciences* 9 (2005): 585–594.

4. John S. Morris, Arne Öhman, and Raymond J. Dolan. "Conscious and unconscious emotional learning in the human amygdala." *Nature* 393 (1998): 467–470.

5. David Rock. "SCARF: A brain-based model for collaborating with and influencing others." *Neuroleadership Journal*, no. 1 (2008): 1–9.

6. Paul J. Whalen. "The uncertainty of it all." *Trends in Cognitive Sciences* 11 (2007): 499–500.

7. Naomi I. Eisenberger, Matthew D. Lieberman, and Kipling D. Williams. "Does rejection hurt? An fMRI study of social exclusion." *Science* 302 (2003): 290–292.

8. Golnaz Tabibnia and Matthew D. Lieberman. "Fairness and cooperation are rewarding: Evidence from social cognitive neuroscience." *Annals of the New York Academy of Sciences* 1118 (2007): 90–101.

CHAPTER 4

1. Carolyn H. Declerck, Christoph Boone, and Bert De Brabander. "On feeling in control: A biological theory for individual differences in control perception." *Brain and Cognition* 62 (2006): 143–176.

2. Annie M. Bollini, Elaine F. Walker, Stephan Hamann, and Lisa Kestler. "The influence of perceived control and locus of control on the cortisol and subjective responses to stress." *Biological Psychology* 67 (2004): 245–260

3. Heinrich Böll. "Anecdote concerning the lowering of productivity." Pages 628–630 in H. Böll, *The Stories of Heinrich Böll*, trans. L. Vennewitz (Evanston, IL: Northwestern University Press, 1995).

CHAPTER 5

1. Carol Craig. *Confidence.* Centre for Confidence and Well-Being (2006), http://www.centreforconfidence.co.uk/flourishing-lives .php?p=cGlkPTQ4MA.

2. K. Anders Ericsson. "Attaining excellence through deliberate practice: Insights from the study of expert performance." Pages 21–25 in M. Ferrari (Ed.), *The Pursuit of Excellence Through Education* (Mahwah, NJ: Erlbaum, 2002).

3. Robert Leamnson. "Learning as biological brain change." *Change: The Magazine of Higher Learning* 32, no. 6 (2000): 34–40.

4. Eric Jensen. Brain-Based Learning: *The New Paradigm of Teaching* (Thousand Oaks, CA: Corwin Press, 2008).

CHAPTER 6

1. Walter Mischel and Nancy Baker. "Cognitive appraisals and transformations in delay behavior." *Journal of Personality and Social Psychology* 31 (1975): 254–261.

2. Roy Baumeister, Kathleen D. Vohs, and Dianne M. Tice. "The strength model of self-control." *Current Directions in Psychological Science* 16 (2007): 351–355.

3. William Williamson and David D. Byrne. "Educational disadvantage in an urban setting." Pages 186–200 in D. T. Herbert and D. M. Smith (Eds.), *Social Problems and the City* (Oxford: Oxford University Press, 1979).

4. Nazanin Derakshan, Sinéad Smyth, and Michael W. Eysenck. "Effects of state anxiety on performance using a task-switching paradigm: An investigation of attentional control theory." *Psychonomic Bulletin & Review* 16 (2009): 1112–1117.

5. Erik M. Altmann, J. Gregory Trafton, and David Z. Hambrick. "Momentary interruptions can derail the train of thought." *Journal of Experimental Psychology: General* 143 (2014): 215–226.

6. Victor M. González and Gloria Mark. "Constant, constant, multi-tasking craziness: managing multiple working spheres." Pages 113–120 in *CHI 2004: Proceedings of the SIGCHI Conference on Human Factors in Computing Systems* (New York: ACM, 2004).

7. Roy F. Baumeister and Kathleen D. Vohs. "Willpower, choice, and selfcontrol." Pages 201–216 in G. Lowenstein, D. Read, and R. Baumeister (Eds.), *Time and Decision: Economic and Psychological Perspectives on Intemporal Choice* (New York: Sage).

8. David Gelles. "The Mind Business." *FT Magazine*, August 24 (2012), http://www.ft.com/cms/s/2/d9cb7940-ebea-11e1-985a-00144feab49a.html.

9. Kirk Warren Brown, Richard M. Ryan, and J. David Creswell. "Mindfulness: Theoretical foundations and evidence for its salutary effects." *Psychological Inquiry* 18 (2007): 211–237.

10. Amir Raz and Jason Buhle. "Typologies of attentional networks." *Nature Reviews Neuroscience* 7 (May 2006): 367–379. doi:10.1038/nrn1903.

11. Michael T. Treadway and S. W. Lazar. "Meditation and neuroplasticity: Using mindfulness to change the brain." Pages 186–205 in R. A. Baer (Ed.), *Assessing Mindfulness and Acceptance Processes in Clients: Illuminating the Theory and Practice of Change* (Oakland, CA: Context, 2010).

12. Richard J. Davidson, Jon Kabat-Zinn, Jessica Schumacher, Melissa Rosenkranz, Daniel Muller, Saki F. Santorelli, Ferris Urbanowski, Anne Harrington, Katherine Bonus, and John F. Sheridan. "Alterations in brain and immune function produced by mindfulness meditation." *Psychosomatic Medicine* 65 (2003): 564–570.

13. Peter Vestergaard-Poulsen, Martijn van Beek, Joshua Skewes, Carsten R. Bjarkam, Michael Stubberup, Jes Bertelsen, and Andreas Roepstorff. "Long-term meditation is associated with increased gray matter density in the brain stem." *Neuroreport* 20 (2009): 170–174.

14. Britta K. Hölzel, James Carmody, Mark Vangel, Christina Congleton, Sita M. Yerramsetti, Tim Gard, and Sara W. Lazar. "Mindfulness practice leads to increases in regional brain gray matter density." *Psychiatry Research: Neuroimaging* 191 (2011): 36–43.

15. Eric M. Miller, Gregory M. Walton, Carol S. Dweck, Veronika Job, Kali H. Trzesniewski, and Samuel M. McClure. "Theories of willpower affect sustained learning." *PLOS ONE* 7, art. e38680 (2012).

CHAPTER 7

1. Wilhelm Hofmann, Maike Luhmann, Rachel R. Fisher, Kathleen D. Vohs, and Roy F. Baumeister. "Yes, but are they happy? Effects of trait self-control on affective well-being and life satisfaction." *Journal of Personality* 82 (2013): 265–277.

2. Rebecca E. Kelly, Alex M. Wood, and Warren Mansell. "Flexible and tenacious goal pursuit lead to improving well-being in an aging population: A ten-year cohort study." *International Psychogeriatrics* 25 (2013): 16–24.

3. Robert P. Spunt, Emily B. Falkand, and Matthew D. Lieberman. "Dissociable neural systems support retrieval of how and why action knowledge." *Psychological Science* 21 (2010) 1593–1598.

4. Elliot Berkman and David Rock. "To achieve your goals, learn how to hack your brain." *Fast Company*, October 10 (2012), http://www.fastcompany.com/3002031/achieve-your-goals-learn-how-hack-your-brain.

5. Elliot Berkman. "Goals, Motivation and the Brain." *Psychology Today*, November 12 (2012), http://www.psychologytoday.com/blog/the-motivated-brain/201211/goals-motivation-and-the-brain.

6. Joseph Nuttin. *Future Time Perspective and Motivation: Theory and Research Method* (New York: Psychology Press, 2014).

7. Daniel L. Ames, Adrianna C. Jenkins, Mahzarin R. Banaji, and Jason P. Mitchell. "Taking another person's perspective increases self-referential neural processing." *Psychological Science* 19 (2008): 642–644.

8. Jason P. Mitchell, Jason, C. Neil Macrae, and Mahzarin R. Banaji. "Dissociable medial prefrontal contributions to judgments of similar and dissimilar others." *Neuron* 50 (2006): 655–663.

9. Malia Mason and David Rock. "The neuroscience of intent." NeuroLeadership Summit, May 10 (2011), http://blog.neuroleadership .org/2011_05_01_archive.html.

10. Viktor Frankl. *Man's Search for Meaning: An Introduction to Logotherapy* (New York: Touchstone Press, 1959, 1962, 1984).

11. Robert Cialdini. *Influence: The Psychology of Persuasion* (New York: Harper Business, 2006 revised edition).

12. Rob McCarney, James Warner, Steve Iliffe, Robbert van Haselen, Mark Griffin, and Peter Fisher. "The Hawthorne effect: A randomised, controlled trial." *BMC Medical Research Methodology* 7, art. 30 (2007).

13. Warner W. Burke. "A perspective on the field of organization development and change: The Zeigarnik effect." *Journal of Applied Behavioral Science* 47 (2011): 143–167.

CHAPTER 8

1. Angela L. Duckworth, Christopher Peterson, Michael D. Matthews, and Dennis R. Kelly. "Grit: Perseverance and passion for long-term goals." *Journal of Personality and Social Psychology* 92 (2007): 1087–1101.

2. Alia J. Crum, Peter Salovey, and Shawn Achor. "Rethinking stress: The role of mindsets in determining the stress response." *Journal of Personality and Social Psychology* 104 (2013): 716–733.

3. Peter L. Broadhurst. "Emotionality and the Yerkes-Dodson law." *Journal of Experimental Psychology* 54 (1957): 345–352.

4. Herbert Benson, *The Relaxation Response* (New York: Harpertorch, 1975, 2000).

CHAPTER 9

1. C. Cian, N. Koulmann, P. A. Barraud, C. Raphel, C. Jimenez, and B. Melin. "Influences of variations in body hydration on cognitive function: Effect of hyperhydration, heat stress, and exercise-induced dehydration." *Journal of Psychophysiology* 14 (2000): 29–36.

2. Philippa Norman. *Healthy Brain for Life* (2014), http://www.healthybrainforlife.com/articles/school-health-and-nutrition/feeding-the-brain-for-academic-success-how.

3. Michael Serra and Thomas B. Shea. "Apple juice stimulates organized synaptic activity in cultured cortical neurons." *Current Topics in Nutraceutical Research* 7 (2009): 93–96.

4. Joanne Cantor. "Is background music a boost or bummer?" *Psychology Today*, May 27 (2013), http://www.psychologytoday.com/blog/conquering-cyber-overload/201305/is-background-music-boost-or-bummer.

5. Diana Deutsch. "Speaking in tones: Music and language partner in the brain." *Scientific American Mind*, July 1 (2010), http://www.scientificamerican.com/article/speaking-in-tones-jul10.

6. Oliver Sacks. *Musicophilia: Tales of Music and the Brain* (Toronto: Borzoi Book, 2007).

7. Daniel J. Levitin. *This is Your Brain on Music* (New York: Dutton, 2006).

CHAPTER 10

1. Kimball Johnson (reviewer). "Coping with excessive sleepiness." WebMD (2012), http://www.webmd.com/sleep-disorders/excessive-sleepiness-10/default.htm.

2. National Sleep Foundation. *National Sleep Foundation White Paper on Drowsy Driving* (Arlington, VA: National Sleep Foundation, 2012), http://drowsydriving.org/2012/11/national-sleep-foundation-white-paper-on-drowsy-driving.

3. Jessica D. Payne. "Learning, memory and sleep in humans." *Sleep Medicine Clinics* 6 (2011): 15–30.

4. Murray W. Johns. "A new method for measuring daytime sleepiness: The Epworth Sleepiness Scale." *Sleep* 14 (1991): 540–545.

5.   William DS Killgore, Thomas J. Balkin, and Nancy J. Wesensten. "Impaired decision making following 49 h of sleep deprivation." *Journal of Sleep Research* 15 (2006): 7–13.

6.   Giada Di Stefano, Francesca Gino, Gary Pisano, and Bradley Staats. *Learning by Thinking: How Reflection Aids Performance.* Harvard Business School NOM Unit Working Paper no. 14-093 (Cambridge: Harvard Business School, 2014).

7.   Tracy A. Bedrosian, Celynn A. Vaughn, Anabel Galan, Ghassan Daye, Zachary M. Weil, and Randy J. Nelson. "Nocturnal light exposure impairs affective responses in a wavelength-dependent manner." *Journal of Neuroscience* 33 (2013): 13081–13087.

CHAPTER 11

1.   E. Luders, A. W. Toga., N. Lepore, and C. Gaser. "The underlying correlates of long-term meditation: Larger hippocampal and front volumes of gray matter." *Neuroimage* 45 (2009): 672–678.

2.   Marcus Raichle, Ann Mary MacLeod, Abraham Z. Snyder, William J. Powers, Debra A. Gusnard, and Gordon L. Shulman. "A default mode of brain function." *Proceedings of the National Academy of Sciences* 98 (2001): 676–682.

3.   Véronique A. Taylor, et al. "Impact of meditation training on the default mode network during a restful state." *Social Cognitive and Affective Neuroscience* 8 (2012): 4–14.

4.   Ruth A. Baer and Jennifer Krietemeyer. "Overview of mindfulness-and acceptance-based treatment approaches." Pages 3–27 in R. A. Baer (Ed.), *Mindfulness-Based Treatment Approaches: Clinician's Guide to Evidence Base and Applications* (Burlington, MA: Academic Press, 2006).

5.   Daniel M. Wegner, David J. Schneider, Samuel R. Carter III, and Teri L. White. "Paradoxical effects of thought suppression." *Journal of Personality and Social Psychology* 53 (1987): 5–13.

6.   William Duggan. "How aha! really happens." *Strategy and Business* 1, no. 61 (2010): 1–5.

7.   Meng Hu, John Kounios, Mark Beeman, and Hualou Liang. "Functional network analysis of insight in resting-state brain activity." Pages 421–425 in *2011 Fourth International Workshop on Advanced Computational Intelligence (IWACI)* (Piscataway, NJ: IEEE, 2011).

8.   Jon Kabat-Zinn and Thich Nhat Hanh. *Full Catastrophe Living: Using the Wisdom of Your Body and Mind to Face Stress, Pain, and Illness* (New York: Random House, 2009).

9.   Jon Kabat-Zinn. *Wherever You Go, There You Are: Mindfulness Meditation in Everyday Life* (New York: Hyperion, 1994).

10. Lesley Jones and Gretchen Stuth. "The uses of mental imagery in athletics: An overview." *Applied and Preventive Psychology* 6 (1997): 101–115.

11. Scott D. Slotnick, William L. Thompson, and Stephen M. Kosslyn. "Visual memory and visual mental imagery recruit common control and sensory regions of the brain." *Cognitive Neuroscience* 3 (2012): 14–20.

12. Robert R. Provine. *Laughter: A Scientific Investigation* (New York: Penguin, 2001).

13. Rod A. Martin and Nicholas A. Kuiper. "Daily occurrence of laughter: Relationships with age, gender, and Type A personality." *Humor: International Journal of Humor Research* 12 (1999) 355–384.

CHAPTER 12

1.   American Association for Retired Persons, AARP.org.

2.   John J. Ratey. *Spark: The Revolutionary New Science of Exercise and the Brain* (New York: Hachette Digital, 2008).

3.   Mirko Wegner, Ingo Helmich, Sergio Machado, Antonio E Nardi, Oscar Arias-Carrion, and Henning Budde. "Effects of exercise on anxiety and depression disorders: Review of meta-analyses and neurobiological mechanisms." *CNS & Neurological Disorders-Drug Targets* 13 (2014): 1002–1014.

4.   Timothy J. Schoenfeld, Pedro Rada, Pedro R. Pieruzzini, Brian Hsueh, and Elizabeth Gould. "Physical exercise prevents stress-induced activation of granule neurons and enhances local inhibitory mechanisms in the dentate gyrus." *Journal of Neuroscience* 33 (2013): 7770–7777.

CHAPTER 13

1.   Matthew D. Lieberman. Social: *Why Our Brains Are Wired to Connect* (New York: Crown Publishing, 2013).

2.   Robin Dunbar. *How Many Friends Does One Person Need? Dunbar's Number and Other Evolutionary Quirks* (London: Faber & Faber, 2010).

3.   Michael Kosfeld, Markus Heinrichs, Paul J. Zak, Urs Fischbacher, and Ernst Fehr. "Oxytocin increases trust in humans." *Nature* 435 (2005): 673–676.

4.   Paul J. Zak. *The Moral Molecule: The Source of Love and Prosperity* (New York: Dutton, 2012).

5.   Sigal G. Barsade. "The ripple effect: Emotional contagion and its influence on group behavior." *Administrative Science Quarterly* 47 (2002): 644–675.

6.   Madelon M. E. Riem, Marinus H. van IJzendoorn, Mattie Tops, Maarten A. S. Boksem, Serge A. R. B. Rombouts, and Marian J. Bakermans-Kranenburg. "No laughing matter: intranasal oxytocin administration changes functional brain connectivity during exposure to infant laughter." *Neuropsychopharmacology* 37 (2011): 1257–1266.

7.   Angelika Dimoka. "What does the brain tell us about trust and distrust? Evidence from a functional neuroimaging study." *MIS Quarterly* 34 (2010): 373–396.

8.   Michael W. Kraus, Cassey Huang, and Dacher Keltner. "Tactile communication, cooperation, and performance: An ethological study of the NBA." *Emotion* 10 (2010): 745–749.

9.   Shelly L. Gable, Harry T. Reis, Emily A. Impett, and Evan R. Asher. "What do you do when things go right? The intrapersonal and interpersonal benefits of sharing positive events." *Journal of Personality and Social Psychology* 87 (2004): 228–245.

10. Steven R. Covey. *7 Habits of Highly Effective People: Powerful Lessons in Personal Change* (New York: Simon & Schuster, 1989, 2004).

CHAPTER 14

1.   Hiehiko Takahashi, Motoichiro Kato, Masato Matsuura, Dean Mobbs, Tetsuya Suhara, and Yoshiro Okubo. "When your gain is my pain and your pain is my gain: Neural correlates of envy and Schadenfreude." *Science* 323 (2009): 937–939.

CHAPTER 15

1.   Charles J. Walker. "Experiencing flow: Is doing it together better than doing it alone?" *Journal of Positive Psychology* 5 (2010): 1–9.

2. Eric S. Fortune, Carlos Rodríguez, David Li, Gregory F. Ball, and Melissa J. Coleman. "Neural mechanisms for the coordination of duet singing in wrens." *Science* 334 (2011): 666–670.

3. Anita Williams Woolley, Christopher F. Chabris, Alex Pentland, Nada Hashmi, and Thomas W. Malone. "Evidence for a collective intelligence factor in the performance of human groups." *Science* 330 (2010): 686–688.

Index